Is There a Future for God's

An
Evangelical
Theology

Henry H. Knight III

Abingdon Press
Nashville

IS THERE A FUTURE FOR GOD'S LOVE?
AN EVANGELICAL THEOLOGY

Copyright © 2012 by Abingdon Press

All rights reserved.

This book is printed on acid-free paper.

Library of Congress Cataloging-in-Publication Data has been requested.

ISBN 978-0-687-66033-9

All scripture quotations unless noted otherwise are taken from the New Revised Standard Version of the Bible, copyright 1989, Division of Christian Education of the National Council of the Churches of Christ in the United States of America. Used by permission. All rights reserved.

12 13 14 15 16 17 18 19 20 21—10 9 8 7 6 5 4 3 2 1

MANUFACTURED IN THE UNITED STATES OF AMERICA

To my parents,
Henry and Mary Knight

CONTENTS

ACKNOWLEDGMENTS

I have been blessed by a number of people who have read this manuscript and offered wise counsel and welcome encouragement. At more than one point along the way, Steven J. Land made valuable observations and pointed me to important resources that greatly strengthened and deepened the argument. Don E. Saliers provided helpful advice that both clarified and enriched my discussion. This book has also benefitted from the insightful comments and suggestions of several theologically astute pastors, including Katherine Bray, John Collins, Laura Guy, Philip Hamner, Robert Maffitt, and Rodney McNeall. I have not only improved this text through their careful reading and advice, I have also grown theologically and spiritually through our conversations over many years. I am grateful beyond words for their friendship and prayers. Finally, I am ever so thankful to my wife, Eloise, for her patient and careful work in preparing this manuscript for submission and for her constant encouragement as it was being written.

INTRODUCTION

Is there a future for love? A casual glance at our world today invites a mixed verdict. On one hand, we could point to the affection found in families and friendship, and the often sacrificial actions by tens of thousands of people to alleviate suffering and combat injustice. Whether love is defined as romantic, filial, or caring, it seems to be doing well. Yet on the other hand, it is just as evident that love is missing from much of life. Families are torn by acrimony, marriages are torn by divorce, friendships are ruptured, and thousands daily die in loneliness. Much of the suffering and all of the injustice in the world is certainly abetted if not caused by the absence of love. The world is not as it should be, and lack of love is a central reason.

In this book I want to focus the question in this way: is there a future in this world for the love revealed in Jesus Christ? The presupposition behind this question is that God, who is love, created a world in which that love would be manifest, most especially in humanity, which was created in the divine image. Clearly that is not the case now: humanity does not reflect that love revealed in Jesus Christ, whether in its relations with God, one another, or the created order. Things are not the way God intended largely because *we* are not the way God intended us to be.

Can we become once again persons who love as God loves? The Christian tradition has consistently answered yes. It has affirmed that at the end of history, the risen Jesus Christ will return to renew the creation so that God's love will reign in absolute fullness. In the meantime, prior to this eschatological conclusion, Christianity has insisted to varying degrees that we can be changed, that we can at least begin to manifest God's love in our lives, and that God's will can at least begin to be done on earth as in heaven.

I am a Wesleyan evangelical. The evangelical tradition, in its classic form with its central teaching of the promise of new birth, is among those that have insisted God can transform hearts and lives such that we are marked by love and other fruit of the Spirit. The Wesleyan tradition, with its teaching on Christian perfection (or perfect love), carries this promise to its fullest extent: love can become the sole governing motivation of our hearts and lives.

Yet these theological claims are often met with incredulity, not only from the outside but also from within evangelical and Wesleyan circles. We are all too familiar with persons who have had conversion experiences, or even a series of intense spiritual experiences, whose attitudes and actions seem sharply at odds with what would be expected of someone who is "dead to sin and alive to God in Christ Jesus" (Rom. 6:11). The fact that Paul is here (as in most of his other letters) exhorting Christians to *be* Christian only places this inconsistency in the New Testament church itself. What do we make of the converted Christian who continues to worship Mammon along with God, or the born-again believer who, as a result of his conversion, abstains from profligate living and treats his wife and children with radically new care and respect yet continues to hold racist attitudes unabated?

It is my belief that God promises us much more than marginal improvement in this life. What I hope to show is both the nature of the new birth—what it is and what it isn't—and the practices in which we participate with the Christian community that open us to God's transforming power and thus to growth in love. In other words, I hope to show that there is indeed a future for love in our world and in this life.

It will perhaps be helpful here to outline the argument in brief. In chapter 1 I discuss what I mean by "evangelical theology." In the process, I try to show the role the new birth plays in the larger evangelical vision of a renewed church faithfully engaged in mission.

The next two chapters examine major obstacles faced, especially in the American context, for receiving and living a new life in Christ. Chapter 2 sketches the modern Enlightenment understanding of freedom as consisting of a lack of constraint on individual choice, which remains the pervasive assumption of our culture today in both its rationalist and romanticist forms. Two case studies on race and consumerism illustrate how this deeply embedded understanding of freedom prevents us from seeing our cultural captivity, thus distorting our vision of the world, whether it is how we see others or how we see ourselves.

Chapter 3 shows how both the technological strand of rationalism and the romanticist kind of individualism continue to flourish in a postmodern culture. It concludes that the romanticist self in the end comes to a spiritual and moral dead end, only able to vigorously assert its own moral preferences while rejecting the imposition of the preferences of others as a constraint on its freedom.

Given our finitude and sin, we neither see our cultural captivity nor desire to escape it. True freedom—freedom to love—must come from outside of ourselves. That is the goal of Chapter 4: to show how God through Jesus Christ reveals the meaning and purpose of life and is present to set us free to live a new life of love. Central to this claim is that it is the particularity of God's revelation in Christ that is the necessary precondition for us to truly know and love God.

Chapter 5 then describes how we know and love God through the transformation of the heart. Central to this work of God are holy affections or tempers—that is, new dispositions, desires, and motivations, the chief of which are love for God and our neighbor. These affections constitute our character and are formed in response to and in imitation of the God revealed in Jesus Christ.

The final two chapters then address how this understanding of new birth and sanctification deals with the obstacles to new life in Christ noted in the earlier chapters. Chapter 6 looks at practices in the life of the church that enable us to remain in relationship with God and avoid the problem of divided hearts. Chapter 7 suggests practices through which God can enable us to see our world and our neighbor with greater clarity, diminishing the effect of our limited perspective and cultural captivity. Thus chapter 6 has as its focus the dispositions of our hearts, whereas chapter 7 is concerned with how we live out those dispositions in the world.

What I hope to show is that the Christian life is indeed grounded in a transformation of the heart brought about through the grace of God. A new birth is not an ending but a beginning. It is an entrance into an ongoing relationship with God that leads to continued growth in love and seeing the world anew. In this way, our hearts increasingly reflect the love of God, and the vision of God increasingly guides our actions. In this way, we find that there is indeed a future for love.

Part I

THE MISSION OF
EVANGELICAL THEOLOGY

Chapter One

THE SHAPING OF EVANGELICAL THEOLOGY

Evangelicals are passionate about sharing the good news of Jesus Christ. They have been ardent participants in spiritual awakenings around the world. They are prime organizers of revivals, evangelistic programs, and Bible studies. They have been quick to use the latest media—newspapers, tracts, magazines, radio, television, video, and now the Internet—to proclaim the gospel. They have launched massive social movements to reform society and have initiated vast missionary movements across the globe.

The reason for all this activity is a conviction that God can transform human lives, relationships, and human society. In a world such as ours, beset with war and injustice, disappointments and heartaches, poverty and hopelessness, and driven by materialism and the pursuit of pleasures that leave life empty and meaningless, to hear that things do not have to be the way that they are is good news indeed. Sins can be forgiven; relationships can be healed; lives can have meaning; and human society can have hope. Indeed, death itself does not have the last word. This good news has its foundation in what God has done in Jesus Christ and what God continues to do through the Holy Spirit.

At the very heart of this divine promise of redemption is love. "God is love" (1 John 4:16); "God's love was revealed among us in this way: God sent his only Son into the world so that we might live through him" (1 John 4:9). God's love is marked by compassion and sacrifice. Yet that does not say enough. It doesn't fully encompass how God incarnate in Jesus reached out in love to tax-gatherers and zealots; Samaritans and centurions; women and children; the sick and the disabled; lepers and those possessed by demons; those dead in sin and those physically dead. It doesn't quite express the love that led to the cross, in which "God proves his love for us in that while we still were sinners Christ died for us" (Rom. 5:8). This is a love that, in the end, *God* defines and does so most fully in the life and death of Jesus Christ. We come to know the full meaning of this love not through theological dictionaries but as we grow in the knowledge and love of God through faith in Jesus Christ and in the power of the Spirit.

It is the joyful task of evangelical theologians to reflect on the nature of this transformation of hearts and lives through the power of this loving redemption in Christ. This book is a contribution to that task. A major thesis is that the central feature of this new life that God gives is love—a love for God, for all persons, and for the creation itself. Because this life is in relation to God, it has a distinctive shape both in response to and in imitation of God's love for us in Christ. This change of heart does not instantly change everything around us but it does transform our dispositions and lives, affect our values and relationships, put us on a journey toward growth, motivate us for ministry, and give our lives meaning. It is an eschatological inbreaking into our hearts and lives.

Yet this claim that God changes hearts and lives is not self-evident. It is not just critics who can find real-life examples that undermine if not discredit the promise of new birth. Christians are also well aware of persons whose lives do not match up with their profession of faith, not only in the high-profile cases of clergy misconduct but also among everyday believers in the pews. It is this disjunction between the claim of conversion and the reality of the life that is lived that is the greatest challenge to the credibility of the gospel. It raises the question of whether we can become persons whose hearts and lives are truly governed by love—whether there really is a future for love in this life.

That is the central question this book seeks to address. It will therefore focus on this divine transformation of the heart: what it is and the difference it makes; impediments to receiving it and living it out, and how they can be overcome. In the process we will discover that a pervasive culturally embedded misunderstanding of human freedom is at the root of much of our failure to both nurture loving dispositions and to act in ways that are genuinely compassionate. We will not be attempting to address every concern or issue. But we will seek a clearer understanding of what new birth and sanctification actually are and to identify spiritual practices that assist persons to both grow in love and live that love with greater faithfulness and effectiveness.

We will begin that examination in earnest in chapter 2. Here, in the remainder of this chapter, I want to look more closely at what is meant by "evangelical theology." This will not only identify more clearly the theological perspective with which I approach this topic but also show the absolutely critical place of the new birth within the evangelical theological vision.

Who Are the Evangelicals?

I am developing a self-consciously evangelical theology. The term *evangelical* has been given to a movement of Christians, mostly Protestant, which has its origins in the religious awakenings of the eighteenth century. Even in its inception it defied strict definition; today, as a global phenomenon, evangelicalism encompasses almost unimaginable diversity.

It is clear from these brief remarks that I reject equating evangelicalism with the "religious right" in America or with "fundamentalism." To be sure, these are segments of the evangelical movement, but they are neither dominant nor definitive. The American media, with its focus on political issues, has been greatly misleading in its assumptions about and depictions of evangelicalism, though this has been partially remedied in recent years.

In *A Future for Truth* I described evangelicalism as a highly diverse movement, which nonetheless has a family resemblance. It was examined from the standpoint of a common set of beliefs—such things as Jesus Christ as incarnate divinity, Lord, and Savior; the authority and inspiration of Scripture; the presence and power of the Holy Spirit; the need for conversion and spiritual growth; and the importance of evangelism—and as a distinctive spirituality.[1] Most of the discussion involved an extended historical argument, showing the interplay of Pietist and scholastic tendencies in producing diverse and at times almost contradictory forms of evangelicalism.[2]

Although in my earlier treatment I began with the Protestant Reformation, I agree with recent historical works that place the inception of modern evangelicalism in the eighteenth-century awakenings.[3] The great tributaries of the Reformation—Puritanism, Pietism, and even to some extent Anglican spirituality—all fed into evangelicalism; it in turn became a massive spiritual river, which had a major impact on the geography of cultures all over the world. It was, at the same time, shaped and domesticated by those cultures and thereby lost some of its original spiritual dynamism. Still, it flows powerfully today, having its most recent impact in the Southern Hemisphere.

Even apart from cultural and racial/ethnic differences, evangelicalism has so many crosscurrents that some question whether it is a useful term at all.[4] The tensions between Calvinists and Arminians within evangelicalism go back to the eighteenth century, whereas the tensions between Pietism and scholasticism go back to the seventeenth century. There have been major disagreements over eschatology, revivalism, the nature of Scripture, the role of women in church and society, charismatic phenomena, economic and political issues, and the church growth movement. Such diversity should encourage modesty in those who would offer definitions.

David Bebbington, with that appropriate modesty, has identified "four qualities" that have characterized evangelicalism: "*conversionism*, the belief that lives need to be changed; *activism*, the expression of the gospel in effort; *biblicism*, a particular regard for the Bible; and what may be called *crucicentrism*, a stress on the sacrifice of Christ on the cross. Together they form a quadrilateral of priorities that is the basis of Evangelicalism."[5] The appeal of Bebbington's definition is that it identifies common elements while not disallowing additional priorities from different segments of the movement nor specifying too precisely the theological beliefs that inform them.

Others have sought to amend Bebbington's proposal by adding to it. Roger Olson would include a "deference to traditional, basic Christian orthodoxy within a higher commitment to the authority of God's Word in Scripture as the norming norm of all Christian faith and practice";[6] Peter Goodwin Heltzel would add "transdenominational populism";[7] and Thomas S. Kidd would include "an increased emphasis on the role of the Holy Spirit in seasons of revival and personal conversion."[8] All of these amendments have merit.

My own approach is to identify three goals or concerns that characterize the theology of evangelicalism. This means that, unlike that of historians, my focus will not be on the movement as such but on its theological aims.

This in turn will set the stage for the chapters that follow.

The Goals of Evangelical Theology

For most of the history of Christianity, theology was reflection on the faith to enable persons to grow as Christians and the church to be faithful in the world. Indeed, as Kilian McDonnell has noted, "Up until the twelfth century theology was not a manner of knowing but a manner of praying,"[9] involving the affections of the heart. Even later, with the advent of more scholastic and systematic theology, theology was still understood as being about a kind of wisdom for knowing, loving, and serving God.[10] It was, as John Wesley would say, more a "practical divinity" than a "speculative divinity."

Evangelical theology has stayed close to the concerns of this tradition. It has most especially been an attempt to maintain the identity and vitality of Christian faith and life in the face of three distinct challenges that first emerged in the eighteenth century. At times, an overemphasis on one of these has led to an impoverishment of the others. Yet, as we shall see, each one is necessary for the integrity of the other two.

The Defense of Orthodoxy

The first of these concerns is *apologetic*: the defense of traditional theological claims against both secular skepticism and attempts by liberal theology to dilute or modify those claims to fit modern sensibilities. Apologetics has been a theological concern since the beginning of Christianity. In 1 Peter 3:15-16 we are urged to "always be ready to make your defense to anyone who demands from you an accounting for the hope that is in you; yet do it with gentleness and reverence." (This last part of the admonition has, sadly, all too often been neglected.)

For evangelicals, it was not the diverse spiritualities of the first century but the emerging secularity of the eighteenth-century Enlightenment that shaped its apologetics. Prior to the seventeenth century, the bias in Western thought had been to have confidence in long-held ideas that had stood the test of time, while those of more recent vintage faced suspicion. The Enlightenment turned this on its head. The philosophy of Descartes and Locke, and the science of Bacon and Newton, challenged inherited notions with the explanatory power of their newer ideas. Science in particular began to provide explanations of natural phenomena that were more satisfactory than those of the past. Disease, crop failures, and natural disasters were understood not as the judgment of God or as being caused by demonic influence but as the result of natural processes that could be understood and, perhaps, predicted or prevented through human ingenuity. The theories of ancient authorities, previously assumed to have stood the test of time, were being swept away by those that were new and progressive.

This was a revolution in thought that promised a future of progress and prosperity. It was based on moving the authority or what is true from Scripture and tradition to the reason and experience of the autonomous individual. The methodological doubt at the heart of the Enlightenment project would in fact scrutinize both Scripture and Christian tradition themselves, with unsettling results for theological orthodoxy.

Initially, many Christian intellectuals sought to use the new Enlightenment methods to confirm orthodox belief. Indeed, many scientists were in awe of the handiwork of God in designing a universe of natural laws. But by the eighteenth century, more and more thinkers began to raise arguments against central elements of the Christian tradition, including the Incarnation, resurrection, miracles, and the authority of Scripture. In response, some Christian intellectuals developed a more modern or liberal version of Christianity. The deists of the eighteenth century were the first sign of things to come; the nineteenth-century liberals, with their emphasis on divine immanence within the ordinary processes of nature and history, would come to dominate the theological world at the beginning of the twentieth century.

Evangelicals saw liberal theology, however well intentioned, not as a modern version of the Christian faith, but instead as the abandonment of those beliefs essential to Christian identity. Evangelicals could be distinguished from liberals by seeing how each reacted to an emerging dualism, assumed by post-Enlightenment thinkers, between "fact" and "faith," which was itself related to the dualism between "object" and "subject." The prevailing assumption was that "fact" was composed of empirically verifiable, universally held objective truths, whereas "faith" consisted of things subjectively believed or experienced but unable to be publicly verified. Thus science dealt with objective facts; religion with subjective faith.

Much of liberal theology was happy with this fact/faith distinction, for among other things it meant that no matter what claims of orthodox Christianity turned out to be factually untrue, their faith would remain untouched. They were more likely to see historic beliefs such as incarnation and resurrection to be contextual expressions of subjective faith than as the ground and reason for faith. Evangelicals were unhappy with how this fact/faith dualism had relegated Christianity to the (presumably less true) "faith" side. For evangelicals, incarnation and resurrection were not simply among a number of ways faith could be expressed; they were the nonsubstitutable ground of Christian faith. To deny these was to deny Christianity itself.

Evangelical theologians developed two overall apologetic strategies, each containing within it a variety of approaches. One strategy was to deny the fact/faith dualism itself by reframing objective reality within the purposes and activity of God. A second was to accept the dualism but seek to rationally demonstrate Christian claims to be publicly verifiable truth, belonging on the "fact" side of the dualism.

Jonathan Edwards and John Wesley, the leading theologians of the eighteenth-century awakening, illustrate the first approach. Both were aware of the direction the new intellectual currents were flowing and both were determined to counter them. They did this not by rejecting the new learning but by reimbedding it within the larger revealed purposes and activity of God. Avihu Zakai describes Edwards's goal as the "reenchantment of the world by demonstrating the infinite power of God's absolute sovereignty in both the 'order of nature' and the 'order of time.'"[11] The deists had exiled God outside the creation and then sought to explain everything within the creation through natural causation. Although their theologies were different at crucial points, both Edwards and Wesley argued that the natural world and human history are best understood as interplays of divinely created natural processes and divine and human agency. That is, our understanding is deficient if it does not recognize ongoing divine activity.

Central to their theologies is the new birth and the occurrence of religious awakenings. Post-Enlightenment thinkers seek the full explanation of these phenomena through natural means, looking, for example, for the psychological reasons for conversion experiences or the socio-historical factors that lead to an awakening. Neither Wesley nor Edwards discount those factors. What they deny is that they constitute a full explanation of the phenomena. The failure of post-Enlightenment accounts of things like conversions and awakenings is because of their ignoring the presence and power of God. There is a larger reality within which nature, history, and humanity must be placed in order to be fully and accurately understood.

How, then, does one know this larger reality? It is certainly revealed in Scripture. But Wesley and Edwards add a second, complementary element to their apologetic: a "spiritual sense" epistemology. Drawing on both Christian tradition and eighteenth-century thought, they understand faith to be a "spiritual sense" that enables us to know—that is, to directly experience—the reality of God. It is important to note what they do not mean by an experiential faith. For Edwards and Wesley experience is not private and individualistic (and hence not unverifiable by being purely "subjective"). To know God through faith is to encounter a God who is other than us ("objective"), analogous in some ways with how we know another person.[12]

Without this faith, which is itself given by God, we do not experience this divine reality and may conclude that if there is a God, that God is removed from the world. It inclines us to reason from natural factors alone. No wonder the deists and other "rational" thinkers, lacking this faith, dismissed conversions and awakenings as mere religious enthusiasm, the result of overheated imaginations. But with faith we know the "spiritual world" (as Wesley put it)[13] and can therefore reason from a more comprehensive experience of reality.

There is nonetheless public evidence that Edwards and Wesley use to defend the genuineness of conversions and awakenings. Edwards early on notes the change in the lives of those truly converted and in the town of Northampton itself following the awakening;[14] later he shows a key sign of holy affections to be active love manifested in human life.[15] Wesley is even more emphatic, seeing the renewal of the heart and life in love as the central evidence of the gospel, drawing the attention of nominal Christians and non-Christians alike.[16] As we shall see, this embodied apologetic is linked to the other evangelical concerns to be discussed below.

In addition to arguing from its effects on lives and communities, Wesley also understood Christian experience to be verifiable in another sense. His frequent use of "experimental" faith (where we would expect the term "experiential") was an invitation to persons to test the promises of the gospel in their own lives. They could then discover for themselves and give public witness to what others had discovered and shared with them.[17]

In the nineteenth century, the conservative Calvinists at Princeton developed a quite different apologetic. Theologians such as Charles Hodge and Benjamin Warfield drew upon both an earlier Protestant scholasticism and the common-sense philosophy of the Scottish Enlightenment to defend the inerrancy of Scripture against liberal and secular critics. The goal of this apologetic was to make a rational argument—that is, to argue on Enlightenment grounds—that Christianity is based on objective truth. Christian truth-claims belong as much as science or social science on the "fact" side of the fact/faith dualism. Faith itself is grounded in rationally defensible factual claims.

There are many varieties of this rational apologetic. Some examine evidence to demonstrate that the Bible is without error, hence trustworthy. Some make a historical case for miracles or the Resurrection. These approaches are often called "evidentialist." A twentieth-century alternative, presuppositionalism, argues that Christianity is the only internally consistent system of belief.[18] But whether evidentialist or presuppositionalist, the goal is the same: to make a rational case for orthodox Christianity by removing intellectual objections to, and demonstrating the truth of, traditional Christian claims. This in turn makes faith in Jesus Christ possible for the post-Enlightenment mind.

My own preference is for the apologetics of Edwards and Wesley. My use of the term *apologetics* for that approach will seem to some a bit unusual—it suggests that the best defense of traditional orthodoxy lies more in thinking of the world in light of God's revelation and experiencing the reality of God than in making a rational case for orthodoxy. My point is that while the content of theology should not be bound by nontheological criteria, it must nonetheless speak with clarity to a contemporary world. It may be that, in the end, the best defense is a good proclamation—and an encounter with a God so transformative that one is unable to look at the world in the same way as before.

The Renewal of the Church

A second major evangelical concern has been *transformational*: to work for the renewal of the church, primarily through inviting persons to enter a life-transforming relationship with God through Jesus Christ. Whereas the apologetic concern was to defend orthodoxy against secular and liberal critics, the concern here is to proclaim a new life in Christ over against a dead orthodoxy and nominal Christianity.[19]

The roots of this evangelical concern lie with the Pietists of the seventeenth century. Pietists belonged to state churches, whose members were baptized and professed historic Christian beliefs. The problem as they saw it was that too many people understood the gospel as offering forgiveness without a transformed life, the assurance of heaven in the end without living a new life in the present.

The Pietist strategy, developed by the German Lutheran Philipp Jakob Spener in the seventeenth century, was twofold: proclaim the need for a new birth to those in the church, and create lay-led small groups to further prayer, the study of Scripture, and spiritual conversation. The goal was the encouragement of an expectant faith open to God's transforming work in human lives and active participation in structured small groups designed to enable Christian growth and discipleship. In addition to these two elements, Spener's disciple, August Hermann Francke, added two more. First, Francke founded a host of institutions to promote a wide range of social, educational, and evangelistic ministries. Second, to Spener's goal of renewing the church Francke added that of sharing the gospel with non-Christians throughout the world. These four emphases—the new birth, small groups, organized social and educational ministries, and world mission—would have a huge impact on the eighteenth-century awakening.[20]

That awakening consisted of a diverse set of participants, unified by their desire to proclaim the new birth and to renew the church. One of these, the Moravian Brethren, led by Count Nikolaus von Zinzendorf, was a branch of Pietism that promoted new birth, small groups, and world mission. They in turn influenced a number of other evangelical leaders, most especially John and Charles Wesley.[21]

A second group of participants were parish clergy in America (such as Edwards), Scotland, and England (both dissenters and Anglican). The model here is the renewal of one's parish, not only transforming the congregation as such but the wider community as well. There was also a commitment by some to send missionaries into unchurched areas.[22]

A third collection of participants were the Methodists, whether Calvinist (George Whitefield) or Wesleyan. These were marked by itinerant preachers, both ordained and lay, who ignored parish boundaries in order to bring the message of new birth to people. They emulated the Pietists in creating institutions for a wide range of ministries and in their commitment to world mission. The Wesleyans had in addition a highly developed pattern of small groups for conversion and growth, and used laywomen as well as laymen as group leaders and even as preachers. The Wesleyans also emphasized holiness of heart and life, or sanctification, as the heart of salvation, with justification and the new birth as the entryway into that new life.[23]

Wesley speaks for many in the awakening when he gives this account of the "principles and actions" of his Methodists:

> We see—and who does not?—the numberless follies and miseries of our fellow creatures. We see on every side either men of no religion at all or men of a lifeless, formal religion. We are grieved at the sight, and should greatly rejoice if, by any means, we might convince some that there is a better religion to be attained, a religion worthy of God that gave it. And this we conceive to be no other than love: the love of God and of all mankind; the loving God with all our heart and soul and strength, as having first loved *us*, as the fountain of all the good we have received and of all we ever hope to enjoy; and the loving every soul which God hath made, every man on earth, as our own soul.[24]

The emphasis on a heart *filled* with love is distinctly Wesleyan, but the desire to convince non-Christians and nominal Christians that there is a new life that they can receive would encompass all segments of the awakening.

The concern for the renewal of the church continued in nineteenth- and twentieth-century revivalism, whose call for conversion often seemed to be aimed as much at those on church rolls as at the unchurched. But a much more focused attention to church renewal was found in the holiness movement, an interdenominational appropriation of the central Wesleyan theme of sanctification. Although the holiness movement contained a number of theologies (from radicalized Wesleyanism to Calvinist-Wesleyan hybrids) and used a range of terms for the desired experience ("entire sanctification"; "Christian perfection"; "second blessing"; "the higher Christian life"; "the victorious life"; "the baptism of the Holy Spirit"), all pointed to the need for a further, subsequent work of God's grace in the lives of believers. The goal of this further work, whether gradual or instantaneous, was the transformation of the heart, including purification from sin and maturing in fruit of the Spirit such as love.

The irony of renewal movements is that so often they ultimately leave the body they sought to renew to form new denominations, aided by the very structures and institutions they had formed to renew the church. Thus Methodists left the Church of England; many holiness bodies in turn left Methodism or other denominations.[25] Sometimes the departures were because of a desire for a "pure" church; often they were the result of strong opposition by those in the home denominations who saw no need for renewal.

Both the desire for renewal and the formation of yet more denominations are shown in pentecostalism,[26] which emerged out of the holiness movement at the beginning of the twentieth century. Pentecostals emphasized the baptism of the Holy Spirit as an empowerment for ministry subsequent to either conversion or entire sanctification. Through this empowerment believers received gifts of the Spirit that strengthened the fellowship and equipped all Christians for ministry and mission.

By the middle of the twentieth century Christians in both mainline Protestant and Roman Catholic churches were experiencing this empowerment by the Spirit. Called "the charismatic movement" or "neopentecostalism," the charismatics sought to remain in their denominations and renew them. Again, organizations and ministries were formed to encourage renewal, and to date most have remained within their parent denominations.[27] However, in the 1970s a number of independent charismatic associations and protodenominations were formed, drawing some charismatics away from their home denominations.[28]

Pentecostalism and its charismatic offspring have become the dominant form of evangelicalism around the world. Fully one-fourth of all Christians today are Pentecostal/charismatic; in 1900 there were almost none. For all their distinctiveness, these newer movements still show continuity with their eighteenth-century ancestors—an emphasis on new life through the power of the Holy Spirit, the creation of small groups and other structures to renew the church and encourage Christian growth, the empowerment of the laity, and involvement in a range of outreaching ministries.

Underlying all of this is one further factor: a sense of the immediacy of God's presence and power in human lives and in our world. There is confidence in and testimony to the transforming power of God. This is not only the precondition for new birth, sanctification, and empowerment but also for God's mission in the world, to which we now turn.

Participating in God's Mission

A third major concern of evangelicalism has been *missional*: to share the good news of Jesus Christ with the world. Although the focus has been on evangelism—inviting persons to accept the good news, forming Christian communities, and nurturing persons in the faith—there has also been a massive movement to meet the human need for food, shelter, health care, and education. More recently there has also been a growing emphasis on caring for the environment. This missional concern seeks especially to turn the attention of inward-looking churches outward, toward their neighbor in need and the creation itself.

The phrase "participating in God's mission" (*missio Dei*) is a bit of an anachronism, as this way of characterizing mission only became common in the twentieth century.[29] But the concept would be familiar to many eighteenth-century evangelicals. Both Edwards and Wesley, for example, saw God as actively enlisting persons to further a divine plan for humanity; both saw awakenings as works of God. Whereas nineteenth-century evangelicals did tend to highlight human effort more, emphasizing how God works *through* the church, the late-twentieth-century vision is of being empowered and led by the Spirit to *join* God's ongoing work in the world.

When the term *missions* is used, it often refers to cross-cultural missions, where a missionary from the church in one culture goes to people of a different culture to share the gospel and engage in a range of compassionate ministries. The term *mission* implies that and more—it refers to the entire evangelistic and social outreach of the church as it participates in God's own mission to the world. Historically, as we have already seen, evangelicals have been highly involved in mission and especially passionate about evangelism.

The roots of this go back at least to August Francke's Pietism with its broad range of social ministries and vision for world evangelism. In the eighteenth century the Moravian Brethren sent hundreds of missionaries across the globe. They were interdenominational in spirit and had an impact out of proportion to their size. Missions were central to their identity, as witnessed by a twenty-four-hour prayer vigil for missions—a vigil that continued uninterrupted for more than a century.

Another important impetus to mission was Jonathan Edwards's *Life of David Brainerd* (1749), the story of a deeply committed missionary to Native Americans that inspired generations of evangelicals. The eighteenth century also witnessed the emergence of mission societies among Baptists, Anglicans, and others.

The explosion of mission activity in the nineteenth century eclipsed all of this activity. Interdenominational benevolent societies promoted social and evangelistic ministries at home and abroad. This continued in the twentieth century with the international Lausanne Committee for World Evangelization as well as a plethora of regional associations and parachurch organizations such as World Vision, Youth with a Mission, InterVarsity Christian Fellowship, and Campus Crusade for Christ.

This brief sketch is only suggestive of a rich and complicated history.[30] Two issues that arise out of it are contextualization and pragmatism. Today, the need to be sensitive to cultural context is taken for granted. In the nineteenth century, the understanding of other cultures was often too superficial and was further complicated by an unwarranted sense of the superiority of Western culture that the Enlightenment encouraged. No theology of mission today that does not give adequate attention to the contextualization of the gospel is credible.[31]

There has also been a tension between faithfulness to inherited tradition and methodological pragmatism. Evangelicals in their impatience with denominational structures and their urgency to be about the Lord's work have been quick to develop new parachurch structures and to adopt uncritically the methods from the world of business and marketing. This is not to say that nondenominational ministries are always unwarranted or that there is nothing to learn from the world at large. But those approaches and lessons need to be kept in tension with the deep and rich theological traditions to avoid superficiality or unintended consequences. The sometime critique that evangelicals lack a strong ecclesiology may be responding to this pragmatic tendency.

One result of three centuries of world evangelism is that the demographic center of evangelicalism is no longer Europe or America but rather Asia, Africa, and Latin America. The decline of Christianity in Europe and North America is being met by a new generation of missionaries from the Southern Hemisphere and eastern Asia, deeply committed (as evangelicals are) to sharing the good news of Jesus Christ. More culturally sensitive but every bit as passionate as the Western missionaries of the past, they are the latest wave of evangelical cross-cultural missionaries.

The Shaping of Evangelical Theology

If theology is understood as contemporary reflection on the beliefs and practices of the Christian community in light of God's revelation, then evangelical theology will necessarily be shaped by these concerns for apologetics, renewal, and mission. The exact shape of theology and practice will be significantly determined by how these concerns are related one to another.

I am arguing for their integration such that no one of them can be properly addressed without attention to the other two. This has not always been the assumption of evangelical theologians or practitioners. The lack of integration has proved detrimental to both understanding and witness, and will only be more so in a postmodern culture. Let me suggest how each one necessarily involves the others.

The apologetic concern, at its best, will give an account to the contemporary world of who God is and what God has done in creation and redemption based on God's revelation. This is essential for shaping the renewal of persons and communities, and to direct missional outreach. At the same time, unless apologetic theology takes account of actual transformed lives and communities, and the reality of missional experience, it can become too abstract and perhaps unaware of how culture can shape our thinking and understanding in ways contrary to the gospel.

The concern to renew the church, at its best, will paint a theological portrait of both the church as a living community and the Christian life, and will encourage the expectant faith necessary to receive the life that God offers. This leads to an embodied apologetic and a motivation for mission. At the same time, unless renewal theology is grounded in God's revelation through Scripture and tradition, and thinks concretely of persons and churches in mission, it can become too individualistic or inward and perhaps unaware of how culture can shape our experience and desires in ways contrary to the gospel.

The missional concern, at its best, will provide a vision of what God is doing in the world. This is essential for a full understanding of the character and promise of God as well as how persons and churches live out the Christian life in the world. At the same time, unless missional theology is grounded in God's revelation and thinks concretely about the nature of the new life God gives, it can become too pragmatic or grounded elsewhere and perhaps unaware of how culture can shape our goals and actions in ways contrary to the gospel.

The apologetic, renewing, and missional concerns are related to another trio of broader terms that shape the theological task. The apologetic concern is to defend *orthodoxy*, or "right belief." Although this is the normal and correct definition of orthodoxy, what is sometimes missed is that *ortho doxa* also means "right glory" or "right praise." Orthodoxy thus not only entails defending the faith but also proclaiming and celebrating it rightly in worship. Unless we worship the triune God, and Jesus Christ as both Lord and Savior, we are not offering "right praise" to God.

The missional concern to become actively involved in

God's work in the world calls us to *orthopraxy*, or the faithful practice of our faith enabled by critical reflection. In the early church, orthodoxy encompassed the entirety of belief and practice, but by the medieval period orthodoxy became limited to referring to doctrinal correctness. In the 1960s, liberation theologians coined the term *orthopraxis*, arguing that theology shapes practice, but how we live our faith in the world shapes our theology. They sought to account for the tendency of ecclesiastical bodies to acquiesce in poverty and injustice even though doctrinally orthodox. They argued that it is in faithful practice, involving working for justice for the oppressed, that one comes to understand God's revelation more fully.

Evangelicals have rightly grounded their theology in God's revelation as authoritatively witnessed in inspired Scripture. But all too often this has been seen as a one-way movement from Scripture to practice, forgetting that what mediates this move is our interpretation or understanding of Scripture. To take orthopraxy seriously—as I think John Wesley did, though without using the term—is to be open to how our practice can illumine our understanding of Scripture and hence our theology.

Many theologians, without necessarily adopting the methodology of liberation theology, have sought to integrate orthopraxy with orthodoxy. Yet for a number of Wesleyan and Pentecostal theologians, this dual emphasis remained inadequate. What was missing was *orthopathy*, or "right experience," a term that would encompass the evangelical concern for a renewed heart and church. They did not always mean the same thing or even use the same term,[32] but each sought to add Christian experience as a third element, shaped by and shaping the other two.

As with orthopraxy, evangelicals did not want orthopathy to lead to the abandonment of God's revelation in Scripture as determining their theology. Not every experience is "right experience." But at the same time, they wanted to draw upon Christian experience as a source for understanding Scripture. How we think about the God of the Bible, and how we see the world in light of God's revelation, is shaped by our experience of God through Scripture, prayer, sacrament, and service, even as it is shaped by doctrine and practice.

Evangelicals who see their theology as shaped by these three elements are not relativizing Scripture. What they are doing is showing how God uses and illumines Scripture as we live out the Christian life in the world. The integration of orthodoxy, orthopraxy, and orthopathy is a way of describing the dynamic by which the Holy Spirit enables us to think and live scriptural Christianity.[33]

My earlier book, *A Future for Truth*, was centered on apologetic concerns and the faithful proclamation of orthodoxy in a postmodern world. This book will be focusing on the concern for renewing the church through transforming the human heart and therefore will be giving a description of orthopathy. It will do so, however, in concert with the apologetic and missional concern and by taking account of the shaping role of both orthodoxy and orthopraxy. The way I do this will be evident in the chapters that follow.

I have already alluded to the content of the renewed Christian church and life as love. The God who gives this life is not any god, but the triune God. The love God gives is not any love, but that in response to and shaped by God's love revealed in the life, death, and resurrection of Jesus Christ. This God will not be considered here as one of a number of potential human expressions of some deeper experience of the divine but as the very particular God of Israel and the church, who creates all that is and enters history to redeem.

In the same way, the Christian life and community and the mission of God in the world are not simply expressions of a more general good or moral life. They are instead the very distinctive life, community, and mission brought about by God in and through Jesus Christ, and they are expressions of the eschatological life that is being even now manifested through the Holy Spirit and will come in fullness with the return of Jesus Christ.

It is this particularity of the Christian life that will be the central theme of all that follows.

Part II
FREEDOM AND LOVE

Chapter Two

THE MODERN QUEST FOR FREEDOM

Salvation implies a kind of freedom, which one receives as a gift from God. It is a freedom from the sin that holds us in bondage—a freedom that, because of that bondage, we could not attain on our own. It is a freedom to live a new life characterized by such fruit of the Holy Spirit as faith, hope, and love. Such freedom is only possible when a person is transformed by God.

But this is a very particular understanding of freedom, which presupposes a set of claims about the character and mission of God and the human condition, among others. It is not the dominant understanding of freedom in the

Western world today. It is this latter view of freedom that has done so much to shape Western culture and has influenced Christian theology and practice, including that of evangelicals. It can serve as a powerful obstacle to receiving and living a new life in Christ.

I will first offer a brief but I hope fair sketch of this modern understanding of freedom and its corresponding view of the self. Then we will examine some ways that this modern view, because of its pervasiveness in Western culture, has compromised evangelical faith and witness.

Freedom in Modernity

By *modernity* I simply mean the culture that emerged in the Western world during the seventeenth century, spawned by the Enlightenment. Its roots were of course earlier, and it initially was a movement within the intellectual elites of Europe. But those intellectuals were both responding to and shaping changes in the culture at large. What they began in the seventeenth century had by the nineteenth resulted in a massive shift in cultural values and assumptions. Today, after four centuries, there are signs that another large-scale cultural shift is under way. Even so, at this moment the culture of modernity remains the dominant ethos for most people in the West.

A central feature of the culture of modernity is its understanding of freedom. Prior to the Enlightenment, persons were understood to be free if they were able to be that which they essentially are (or were created to be), according to the place of humanity in a larger natural order (or in the will of God). With the Enlightenment, freedom became a characteristic and right of the self as such, apart from God or the natural order. To be free was not to be rid of all impediments that would prevent conformity to an external norm or intrinsic essence, but to exercise freedom of choice, free of external constraint.

Morality, then, is grounded in the autonomous individual self. The assumption was not only that each person possesses a capacity to make moral decisions but also, when truly free to exercise that capacity, possesses the inclination to do so. This optimistic view of human nature undergirded a universal affirmation of human dignity and respect.

We can understand their passion for this form of freedom by seeing the world they sought to leave behind. It was a world of constraint—on thinking and living; on spiritual values and material possibilities; enforced by government and church. Hierarchical societies made sharp distinctions between aristocrat and commoner, male and female, clergy and laity. Each person was born into a social class and expected to remain in that class. Christianity and culture were so intertwined that faithfulness could not be easily conceived except in terms of a hierarchical social order in which authority was located at the top.

Although many early Enlightenment figures were devout Christians, there was a gradual moving away from traditional Christianity, first in deism and finally in agnosticism. This was because many concluded that constraint on human freedom (and a concomitant denigration of human dignity) is a necessary corollary to belief in God.

Philosopher Charles Taylor argues that many were led to abandon theism entirely because they were convinced we could only be genuinely free, moral beings apart from God.[1] Unlike their forebears who thought that "the spiritual dimension of their lives was incomprehensible if one supposed there is no God,"[2] moderns could easily envision a moral life entirely based within the capacities or nature of the self. Thus not only was God unnecessary to a moral life but also many found belief in God to be detrimental. We could not be free to be moral in ourselves if we were constrained by a moral authority external to ourselves.

Taylor identifies another significant motive for rejecting religion, one highly relevant to the argument of this book. This is affirmation of ordinary life,[3] which Taylor calls "one of the most powerful ideas in modern civilization." It originated with the Protestant reformers, who rejected the prevailing notion that clergy and those in religious orders who had renounced marriage and everyday life lived their lives closer to the divine pattern than did ordinary Christians. The reformers and their Puritan heirs denied any hierarchy of the more or less religious, hold-ing all are equally sinners and all are saved by grace alone. They did not deny the divine calling to sanctification but insisted that one can live a sanctified life in one's family and vocation.

It is this holding on to sanctification that the heirs of the Enlightenment eventually came to reject. To use an external standard claimed to be from God to measure each person's faithfulness inevitably creates a new hierarchy of the more or less sanctified. It undermines the equal respect due to all persons by refusing to honor the lives and values freely chosen by each individual.

Beginning in the late eighteenth century, this modern commitment to individual freedom developed two com-peting interpretations, both of which continue to power-fully shape Western culture. The story of their historical development and variant expressions is complex.[4] What I will do here is again offer sketches of their central features.

The *rationalist* strand is linked to the beginning of the Enlightenment and was given its initial shape by such figures as René Descartes and John Locke. For all their differences, both had great confidence in the ability of hu-man reason, when objectively examining the world free of prior beliefs and assumptions (what Taylor calls "dis-engaged" reason),[5] to discover the truth. In the beginning they sought not to abandon Christianity but to ground it more securely through reason and (for Locke) experience; later figures would find Christianity irrelevant or incompatible with the conclusions of reason.

Robert Bellah and his colleagues have termed the American cultural expression of this rationalist strand "utilitarian individualism," with Benjamin Franklin as the representative figure. Because Franklin was committed to personal success, Bellah argues that he valued America for providing a "chance for the individual to get ahead on his own initiative." Bellah's critique is that for many after Franklin "the focus was so exclusively on individual self-improvement that the larger social context hardly came into view."[6] That is, the individualism was so determinative that it became difficult to even see culture except as a collection of fundamentally free and independent individuals. As we shall see, this has had a detrimental effect on Christian discipleship, including especially that of evangelicals.

But besides the myth of the independent, self-made individual, the rationalist strand has shaped culture in another way. It understands reason to be instrumental—through a rational understanding of both society and nature it seeks to manipulate or control them, and through science and technology to advance human society. Indeed, human dignity is at least partially linked to the triumph of reason over nature. Think of the great advances in the prevention and cure of disease, or in the production of food, or in transportation, or in genetic "technology"—or think of Franklin's lightning rod. We call these "advances" because we take for granted that they have contributed to human betterment. Even where there have been severe unintended consequences—environmental degradation for example—we assume that greater understanding and advanced technology (cleaner energy, hybrid cars, and so on) will address the problem.

Darell L. Guder and his colleagues see this constantly changing technological society as producing a number of cultural myths. "One is that the new is somehow better and must necessarily replace the old....Another is that what is efficient is most desirable....A third is that there is a technique solution to every problem...if we just work at it with enough intelligence, or long enough."[7] These pervasive myths have also had their impact on evangelical theology and practice.

The second strand is the *romanticist*, which reacted against the atomistic individualism of the rationalists. With its roots in Jean-Jacques Rousseau, romanticism rejected a disengaged, instrumental reason, which objectified nature in order to control it. It aspires (in Taylor's words) to bring "us back in contact with nature," overcome "the divisions between reason and sensibility," overcome "the divisions between people," and create community. In short, it is a call for us to be "open to or in tune with nature in ourselves and outside."[8]

We can see the impact of romanticism in the resistance of some segments of the environmental movement to technology and in the call of most in that movement to see ourselves not as standing over nature but as part of nature. Even more pervasive is the emphasis on self-expression, or living in accordance with our natural impulses, feelings, or sensibilities. Taylor calls this "the expressivist turn": "our access to nature is through an inner voice or impulse" and "we can only fully know this nature through articulating what we find within us"—that is, "its realization in each of us is also a form of expression."[9]

Bellah terms its manifestation in American culture "expressive individualism," with Walt Whitman as the representative figure. Whitman sought a "life rich in experience, open to all kinds of people, luxuriating in the sensual as well as the intellectual, above all a life of strong feeling." Freedom was "the freedom to express oneself, against all constraints and conditions."[10] Expressive individualism continues unabated in contemporary culture, fueled by the entertainment industry and a consumer culture among other things.[11]

I hope it is evident that my own response to this modern quest for freedom in its various forms is not uniformly negative. Most of us welcome the great gains in understanding the world. We value the technological innovations and the increasing ecological awareness. Yet there is also a fear of unintended consequences and an anxiety about a future that we are creating without a common ethical vision. Unease over genetic technology is a case in point. This in turn illumines a deeper ambiguity with the result of this modern freedom of choice. Most want to maximize their own freedom even as they worry about where it will lead.

Evangelicals and Race in America

The worry about where it will lead is legitimate. The American emphasis on individual freedom has at times led evangelicals in directions contrary to the faith they profess and even contrary to their own best intentions. This can be seen most starkly in evangelical responses to race.

Race is a complex issue with a long history involving the interplay of European, African, various Hispanic and Asian, and Native American peoples. Here we shall focus on relations between white and black Americans, looking at a few historical examples and a recent study. Although inadequate as a thorough examination of race, it may serve as a case study to illumine the effects of modern culture on evangelical faithfulness.

America, according to Michael O. Emerson and Christian Smith, is a "racialized society." Marked by low rates of intermarriage, "a racialized society is one where our identities and friendships are shaped by race. In short, it is a society wherein race matters profoundly for differences in life experiences, life opportunities, and social relationships."[12] In such a society racism is not simply a matter of individual prejudice but a subtle set of practices that are "embedded within the normal, everyday operation of institutions." The effects of these practices are very evident to racial minorities but largely invisible to whites.[13]

Their thesis, based on extensive sociological research, is this: while white "evangelicals desire to end racial divisions and inequality, and attempt to think and act accordingly... in the process, they likely do more to perpetuate the racial divide than to tear it down."[14] Their argument lends credence to the oft-repeated criticism of a focus on conversion, that a changed heart doesn't lead to significant social change and indeed may be a distraction from it. If we want to suggest otherwise (as I do) we shall need to attend carefully to their analysis.

We are all immersed in culture, which shapes our perceptions and actions in myriad ways. First, culture largely determines what we take to be "natural" or "normal." In a racialized society, most of the majority race take for granted racial separation and the behaviors that sustain it. Spencer Perkins observes that

> for the most part, integration has been successful only when it could be forced on the white community. Given a choice, it rarely happens. White parents given the choice to send their children to a mostly black school would most likely choose not

to. A white family with the resources to move out of a racially changing neighborhood will usually do so. A white church that can afford to leave the inner city will usually leave. These choices are second nature. I'm not sure if very many white Christians stop to think of the message they are sending to black Christians as they make these decisions.[15]

This agrees with the findings of Emerson and Smith, who argue that "the racialized society is reproduced in everyday actions and decisions. These are seen...as normal and acceptable, at least by white Americans." Thus, "choice and freedom are two of the dominant American values that today maintain the racialized society."[16]

The problem of culture determining what is "normal" is by no means a purely American problem. Amos Yong tells of how for two decades Syrian and Dalit Pentecostals were joined in equal fellowship in churches in India despite the cultural designation of Dalits as untouchable. From the 1920s to 1940s there was shared table fellowship. Dalits were addressed as "brothers and sisters" instead of by their caste names and some moved to positions of leadership in the church.[17] But in the 1950s and 1960s, the inferior job and educational opportunities for Dalits in the larger society led to their being passed over for leadership roles in the church. "By the late 1960s, not only were Dalits a minority among leaders; Syrian Christians were clearly leery of having Dalit pastors because they feared hindering the growth of the church and losing societal status."[18] Intermarriage waned; the use of caste names for Dalits reemerged; segregation and even racism grew. In response to a formal segregation decision by the Syrians in 1971, the Dalits withdrew in 1972 and formed their own Pentecostal denomination.

The story of the Dalits eerily echoes that of African Americans in Methodist and Baptist churches in early-nineteenth-century America. Although initially experiencing a relative equality when compared to the larger culture, in church after church white majorities eventually segregated blacks and kept them from leadership positions. The result was the formation of predominantly black denominations.

We will need to examine why promising countercultural beginnings are so frequently abandoned after a few decades, with a reversion to cultural norms. More important, we will need to find practices that can help prevent a reversion. What is important to note here is that culture itself, as a human product, has fallen into sin, and therefore does not reflect the norms of the kingdom of God. The impact of culture can be a major obstacle to living a Christian life.

In addition to being sinful, culture is also finite—it presents us with a particular and limited perspective. This leads to a second feature of culture: it determines what we see and what we do not see. In the case of race, African Americans are largely able to see the structural inequities that impinge on their lives, whereas most whites do not see them at all. This has led to two strikingly different approaches to race relations among black and white evangelicals.

African American evangelicals like John Perkins began to develop a theology of reconciliation. Believing "racial reconciliation is God's imperative,"[19] they advocated a four-step process toward achieving it. First, they called for close relationships among persons of different races. Second, those persons must recognize social structures that foster inequality and work together to resist them. The two remaining steps enable this. Whites, as the ones who both created and benefit from a racialized society, "must repent of their personal, historical, and social sins." To not repent of historical and social sins would enable them to be "passed on to future generations, perpetuating the racialized system, and perpetuating sin." African Americans must be willing individually and corporately to forgive whites, repenting of any anger and hatred.[20]

Early leaders like Perkins, Tom Skinner, William Pannel, and James Earl Massey tirelessly presented this message of reconciliation to evangelical audiences. A few whites, like Ron Sider, Jim Wallis, and Tony Campolo, responded positively; by the end of the twentieth century their numbers grew significantly.[21] Yet the overwhelming number of white evangelicals did not so much reject the message as not properly understand it. They focused at best only on the initial step of personal relationship.

The reason, according to Emerson and Smith, is that their differing historical and cultural contexts have led to this divergence of perception among blacks and whites. Thus most white evangelicals operate with a different set of "religio-cultural tools" than black evangelicals. Emerson and Smith identify three cultural tools of white evangelicals: "accountable freewill individualism," an emphasis on relationships between persons, and "an inability to perceive or unwillingness to accept social structural influences."[22]

We have seen how individualism and freedom are central features of modern American culture. Emerson and Smith describe white evangelicals as possessing a variant of this, believing "individuals exist independent of structures and institutions, have freewill, and are individually accountable for their own actions."[23] The emphasis on free will is rooted in the strong evangelical commitment to each individual having the freedom to respond to God's offer of salvation, as witnessed in American revivalism. But in contrast to most other Americans, white evangelicals also hold we are accountable for our decisions, most especially to God and God's laws.

Because human nature is fallen, persons need "a personal relationship with Christ." This is the bedrock belief of evangelicals.[24] But white evangelicals transpose this emphasis on relationship to all other aspects of their lives. Hence racism is seen as an individual sin that leads to poor attitudes and relationships; a changed heart will lead to changed relationships, eliminating the racism. There is not only no concept of how social structures might shape poor relationships but also many believe the talk of racism in structures is a way to shift the responsibility away from the sin of the individual.[25] This antistructural bias among white evangelicals that Emerson and Smith depict is the inverse of many theologically liberal Christians' common complaint that talk of personal conversion shifts our attention away from social change.

The extensive research and interviews conducted by Emerson and Smith paint a picture of well-intentioned persons who are unable to address or even understand the impact of social structures on our lives. Put differently, the problem for many is not racism in the heart. It is instead a culturally conditioned freedom that, in its exercise, makes us complicit with racism in society. Yet it is the heart transformed by love that has the disposition and motivation to address social and institutional racism once it has been recognized as the problem that it is. In order to argue for the importance of conversion and a personal relationship with Jesus Christ we will need to account for how personal transformation both is freed from the negative influence of and positively influences social structures. This is a task for a later chapter, but several things should be said here.

The modern legacy of freedom has been an ambiguous gift at best for evangelicals. Certainly using it to proclaim that anyone on his or her own may accept the grace God offers has led racial and ethnic minorities and women to leave or resist unjust social structures, claiming their equal standing before God over against the subordinate roles given them by culture. Emerson and Smith agree, saying that American religion "can serve as a moral force in freeing people" from the control of others. Unfortunately, at the same time it does a poor job of addressing racial divisions or bringing people "together as equals across racial lines."[26] The freedom that enables the one also perpetuates the other.

Thus supposedly free individuals are actually held culturally captive in two ways: what is considered "normal" becomes second nature to persons in a culture; and what we see and do not see is governed by cultural lenses. Evangelicals have rightly resisted the modern claim that each individual discovers morality through the exercise of reason or within his or her own subjectivity, but in insisting on our moral accountability to God most white evangelicals have reduced God's biblical purposes to matters of right choices in personal attitudes and behavior. They have let the modern idea of freedom as choice trump the deeper and more biblical idea of freedom as becoming who we were created to be. Thus, unlike African American and other evangelicals from minority communities, most have had difficulty thinking in terms of either congregational practice or societal structures. The merger of autonomous individualism with evangelicalism has resulted in a kind of syncretism.

The problem is not evangelicalism itself but how it has contextualized the gospel. This is not a purely American problem, as the example of the Dalits shows. But most white American evangelicals construe their faith and their world individualistically, while African American evangelicals think in terms of social structures and practices as well. They have contextualized the gospel in different ways. I believe evangelicals who follow the African American approach have much to teach us.

One clue is evident from Emerson and Smith (as well as Spencer Perkins and Chris Rice): if we overcome racial isolation we will have a better chance for the fullness of new life in Christ to be realized. Whites who are not isolated from African Americans are much more able to see the structural inequalities and to resist the second nature assumptions of a racialized society. We will need to explore Christian practices that can break down this isolation.

Freedom in a Consumer Culture

If anything is symbolic of the individual freedom of late modernity it is the culture of consumerism. The heart of consumer culture is personal choice, free and uncoerced, dictated by nothing more than one's own preference.

Murray Jardine has perceptively traced the emergence of consumer culture in modernity. He argues that premodern societies assumed humans had only a "limited capacity to change their environment" and therefore developed moral principles that encouraged conformity to "an unchanging natural order."[27] In contrast, persons in modernity "have discovered that they have a much greater capacity to understand, control, and even change their environment," both natural and social.[28] The difficulty has been to develop an approach to moral reasoning that provides guidance in this new situation.

It was this freedom to change the environment that ultimately birthed the culture of consumerism. The development of new technologies eventually brought unprecedented material abundance. At the same time, this prosperity, and the capitalist economy that produced it, has left in its wake cultural shifts that undermine our ability to live Christian lives.

In Jardine's account, the first shift occurred when we moved from a premodern to a modern market economy. Premodern people "did just enough work to meet their basic needs and spent the rest of their time on other activities." In modern capitalism, "work becomes the central human activity" and only the most productive companies and persons do well. There is a corresponding shift in the Protestant work ethic. Originally "one labored for the glory of God and the betterment of one's fellow human beings"; the obligation was to be faithful, to do one's best. Now the necessity is to outperform others in order to keep one's job and advance in one's profession.[29] Our value is tied to what we produce, especially in comparison to others. The market has subtly yet powerfully transformed humans' understanding of their own purpose and worth, as well as the purpose of creation.

The move to a postindustrial economy has further changed the cultural landscape. Jardine nicely states how a highly productive economy necessitates a consumer culture:

> As the capitalist system becomes highly productive, it inevitably develops a consumer culture in order to deal with excess production, that is, its production beyond people's basic needs. But in a consumer culture, the old Protestant ethic of self-denial becomes positively dysfunctional. People who practice self-denial make poor customers. ... A consumer culture must teach people to expect immediate gratification of their desires.[30]

We move from primarily seeing ourselves as producers to being consumers, and our evaluation of our lives and their meaning shifts accordingly. This secularized version of the

Protestant work ethic ultimately tends to destroy itself.[31]

John Wesley, on the eve of an industrial economy, saw a similar pattern in the lives of his Methodists: "For whenever true Christianity spreads it must cause diligence and frugality, which, in the natural course of things must beget riches. And riches naturally beget pride, love of the world, and every temper that is destructive of Christianity."[32] It seems, says Wesley, that "true scriptural Christianity has a tendency in the process of time to undermine and destroy itself"[33]—unless Christians faithfully practice self-denial. We can only imagine his reaction to an entire culture shaped by consumerism, in which self-denial and deferred gratification are seen as strange or impediments to self-expression.

In Wesley's day there were a handful of wealthy persons of leisure for whom excess consumption was a cultural obligation, as it provided jobs and income for the working people of the lower classes. In postindustrial capitalism most of us are both workers and consumers, and few of us have much acquaintance with leisure. According to sociologist Robert Wuthnow, "The distinguishing feature of the middle class is its obsession with work and money."[34] Persons are working longer and longer hours. Although many Americans express satisfaction with their jobs, most complain that there is too little time to do the things they want to do, including being with their families. Children especially suffer from their parents' obsession with work,[35] and adults themselves commonly face stress and burn-out.[36] Material abundance has not produced more time for things other than work.

Yet it is consumerism that gives all this work its purpose. While middle-class Americans worry that we are becoming too materialistic, they consistently list "making a lot of money" and having a "comfortable life" as central, motivating values. Wuthnow concludes that "money and material goods have us firmly in their grasp," though "we are painfully reluctant to admit this fact to ourselves."[37] Sam Van Eman, who ministers to college students, finds that the most common reason freshmen give for their chosen field of study is that "it pays well."[38]

Consumer culture promises unprecedented freedom. We can choose from a wide array of options not only products but also lifestyles, and even the image we portray to others. Expressive individualism has seemingly reached its apogee—we can truly "do our thing." And in doing it, we achieve the romanticist goal of expressing who we truly are.

Yet this freedom turns out on a deeper level to be illusory. The culture of advertising, says Jardine, "amounts to a form of subtle tyranny through propaganda" and leads to consumerism as "an unavoidable, all-encompassing way of life."[39] We are free to choose anything—except whether or not to be a consumer.

This means our choices themselves are governed by values that have their origin not in the gospel but in the market or the advertising culture. Robert Wuthnow bluntly describes how little a role religion plays in middle-class choices:

> Asked if their religious beliefs had influenced their choice of a career, most...Christians and non-Christians alike said no. Asked if they thought of their work as a calling, most said no. Asked if they understood the concept of stewardship, most said no. Asked how religion did influence their work lives or thoughts about money, most said the two were completely separate.[40]

There is a need for moral guidance here, yet many resist religion precisely because it represents a moral authority external to the culture and hence is seen as a threat to their freedom. Sometimes this is exacerbated by religion itself. Sam Van Eman says that Christian teaching in his home "provided general moral guidance for *what* we consumed, but overall it did not serve in full capacity regarding *why* and *how* we consumed it."[41] In other words, it may have guided consumer choices but did not invite critical reflection on consumerism itself in relation to God and the meaning and purposes of life.

But since America is also a consumerist society, religion can itself be domesticated by making it a commodity, a matter of private preference. John Stackhouse says religions are a potential threat to consumerism because they "tend to tell people there is more to life than buying and selling." They "bind people together and…encourage them to take their cues in life from texts, traditions, and teachers that often contradict the imperatives of consumerism." Consumerism thus "tries to co-opt religion, to make religion fit into consumerist patterns and convictions." Whatever does not fit is ridiculed, delegitimized, drowned out, or otherwise opposed.[42]

Consumerism has to oppose religious competitors because in itself it cannot deliver either true freedom or genuine moral guidance. It evokes desires and inculcates values in order to sell products but cannot address in any lasting way questions of deeper meaning.

Consumerism tells us we are free—free of traditional restraints, free to do as we choose, free to consume whatever we can afford. As Rodney Clapp says, "Our culture gives us all sort of options, a breadth of freedom never before enjoyed in human history." The problem is that "it gives us no help at all in knowing what or how to choose." What, he asks, are we supposed to do with our freedom? "Can we do anything with it besides exercising it negatively, by going from one car to another, one job to another, one church to another, one spouse to another?"[43]

The impact of all of this on the church and its faithfulness to God is immense. In addition to the problem of Christians living as uncritical consumers and the gospel itself becoming one more commodity (undercutting its purpose to transform the whole of life), I will note two others.

The first is that the current consumer culture makes self-centeredness normal and natural. Advertising works continually to create desire for things we do not need, often by linking products to lifestyle, sexual attractiveness, or being one-up on your competitors. The overall effect is to keep our focus squarely on ourselves—our pleasure, our possessions, our income, our status, and what others think of us. We do not focus on God except as a means to these ends and normally do not focus on our neighbor in need at all. As Van Eman says, "When we enter careers primarily to earn money and establish security and status for ourselves, observers should not be surprised when we thank God but exclude sacrificial giving."[44] Wuthnow calls for both ministry to our middle-class neighbor suffering from stress and burnout, and service to the "desperately needy." For the middle class to share its resources with the poor it "is likely to require genuine sacrifice—a word that has never been popular in economic circles, let alone in American politics."[45] Such sacrifice seems necessary as well if we are to address environmental issues in addition to poverty.

A recent study by Christian Smith and Michael O. Emerson underscored this detrimental effect of our consumer culture upon Christian faithfulness. In examining why Christians in America do not give more money, they concluded it was not because of a lack of resources or an unawareness of human need. Christians in America could, in fact, "increase their giving dramatically" and still "lead perfectly healthy, happy lives." A major reason Christians do not give more generously is because of how consumer culture and the advertising industry shape their perceptions and influence their decisions. The reason, Smith and Emerson found, is because

> consumerism focuses people's attention not on the blessings and abundance in their lives but on all they do *not* possess.... In the process, regardless of their absolute abundance, many or most Christians come to feel a relative deprivation, a sense they do not have all they could, want, or should possess and experience. The system and culture are set up, in other words, to create permanent discontent.[46]

It may seem that the American response to natural disasters is an exception to this pattern. For example, Americans in 2005 responded in massive numbers to aid the victims of the tsunami in Indonesia, Sri Lanka, and neighboring countries, and to aid the victims of Katrina and other Gulf Coast hurricanes. They also gave aid to victims of drought in Niger, of genocide in Darfur (a human-made disaster), and of the immense earthquakes in Pakistan and Haiti. People gave not only money but many also gave their time. Churches and Christian organizations were among those at the forefront of relief efforts. Even after the 2008 recession, people still have given time and money to alleviate victims of tornadoes, hurricanes, war, and drought. Certainly all this is to be celebrated.

But the main point still holds. It is the immensity of these events, along with coverage by the media, which brings all of this human tragedy to our attention. The question is, how much do we focus on the neighbor in need, whether near or far away, apart from these disasters? What is the focus of our lives? Where is our treasure? For that is also where our hearts will be.

A second impact is the loss of community. Because the market seeks to motivate us as individuals to choose the products it offers, it makes it difficult to think in terms of community or of the common good. Indeed, to even speak of community as if it were more than a collection of individuals, or of common good as more than the sum of their individual desires, is experienced by many as an infringement on their freedom. The effect of this on ecclesiology is that it makes terms like "body of Christ" or "people of God" remote; the church itself becomes a collection of individuals who choose to be there because it meets their perceived needs.

Another aspect of this dissolution of social bonds is the contemporary market strategy of targeting groups of consumers with similar demographic characteristics. This "narrowcasting," (as opposed to "broadcasting") has become enormously easy and profitable with the emergence of cable television and the Internet (and the continued vitality of radio), each with media produced for a particular segment of the culture. While this certainly provides an enormous range of options to choose from, it gives us few if any places where diverse subcultures, classes, ethnicities, and perspectives can be heard together. If by our choices we segregate ourselves (or allow advertisers to separate us) from persons who are different, how do we hear their stories or they ours? It diminishes our opportunity and capacity for understanding, empathy, and compassion.

A Promise Unfulfilled

The promise of the Enlightenment, through both its rationalist and romanticist offspring, was freedom for individuals. Persons would no longer be bound by outmoded institutions and ancient traditions but would be free to think for themselves, make their own choices, and give expression to who they really were. As a result, Americans today do have an enormous range of options to choose from, with minimal external constraint on the choices they make.

Yet, as our case studies on race and consumerism have shown, we are far from free. We are held captive by what our culture presents as "normal," and our ability to "see" societal patterns and institutional practices beyond our personal relationships is compromised by an excessive individualism. Moreover, our understanding of ourselves and our world, as well as our central motivations and desires, is shaped by subtle yet powerful influences. Who we really are is increasingly who our culture makes us. Culture has this power precisely because we take so much for granted. We lack an alternative way of engaging the world—a way that will transform our lives enough to give us a way to see how our culture operates; to evaluate it; and, when necessary, to develop a different set of patterns and practices. We also lack occasions to have conversation together about how we live and who we are in light of God's character and purposes.

One answer to this problem is that freedom comes from the outside, from a gracious God who acts to give us a new life and to incorporate us into a community that dwells within the story of God and engages in practices that critically examine our culture. It is there we discover who we really are.

But another approach would disagree. Certainly, it would say, we should expose the hidden narratives of modern culture that subvert the very freedom they promise to give. But the way to freedom is not, then, to come under the sway of an alternative narrative. Rather, it is to critique any and all accounts that claim to provide ultimate meaning. This is the way to freedom that one strand of postmodernism advocates.

Chapter Three

FREEDOM IN POSTMODERN CULTURE

Freedom in Western modernity was understood as the freedom of choice of the autonomous individual. What we chose was grounded in nothing else but our own reasoning or natural desires. We were freed from any arbitrary external authority that might limit that reasoning or deny those natural desires—arbitrary because it was not itself grounded either rationally or empirically.

What we saw in chapter 2 was that this freedom actually creates a vacuum for other, subtler authorities to limit reasoning and inculcate desire. This undermines the Christian life because it either prevents us from fully receiving the new life in Christ or living out that new life.

In John Wesley's terms, it prevents, hinders, or distorts holiness of heart and life. In short, we are not free to be fully Christian.

Postmodernism carries this quest for freedom further by showing the limitations of the universal explanations favored by the Western philosophical tradition. But although one strand of postmodernism attempts to set us free from these universals, it does not set us free from culture itself or the power of the desires and understandings inculcated by culture. That will take a different approach to freedom, one grounded in narrative, communal practices, and the power of God.

The Collapse of Universals

Postmodernism takes with utmost seriousness how persons are both shaped and limited by their contexts. Of course, modernity was not unaware of context. Its strategy was to find an epistemology based on a common human capacity such as reason or experience in order to transcend cultural limitations. In this way it sought to establish universal truth, bring an end to human conflict, and usher in a new era of peace and freedom.

It is this strategy in which postmodernity has lost faith. The postmodern suspicion is that the sort of universal explanations favored by modernity (and Western philosophy more generally) are not the products of a neutral or objective rationality but of persons who are inextricably situated in their cultural contexts. Thus it is said the interest of postmoderns has moved from epistemology to hermeneutics—the question is not "how can we know" but "how can we interpret what we think we know" given the influence of context.

This is a radical change. The Enlightenment confidence in autonomous individuals' reason is replaced by the recognition that the web of communal relationships and cultural understandings in which we find ourselves deeply shapes our thinking. Factors such as ethnicity, gender, social class, and personal and cultural history cannot be bracketed and to some degree cannot be transcended. The Enlightenment project of discovering universal truth seems to have reached a dead end. At worst, postmodernism holds that there is no universal truth to be found; at best, what we have is a range of limited perspectives on that truth.

There are some definite strengths to this emerging postmodernism. It decisively undercuts the modern Western tendency to believe that its own ideas were both universally true and superior to those of others. For example, it makes nonsensical the Western debate in the eighteenth and nineteenth centuries over whether nonwhite races were inferior by nature and incapable of European levels of civilization (the racist view) or whether nonwhite races, with proper education, could someday elevate themselves to the level of Western European civilization (the liberal view). Not only is a debate like this rendered offensive and ludicrous but also postmodernism insists on inviting participation and welcoming contributions from those "others" who heretofore were only objects in Western intellectual thought.

Evangelicals and other conservative Christians can certainly welcome the dethroning of Enlightenment-style universal reason with its inclination to reduce theological claims to natural explanations. Postmodernism makes less room for rational certainty but more room for mystery and explanations not limited to natural or material categories. It might seem that postmodernism would also provide welcome assistance in dealing with the problems outlined in the previous chapter. After all, if our problem is a lack of awareness of our own cultural captivity and human finitude, an approach that recognizes the power of context and the limits of reason should truly set us free.

That indeed is the promise of one strand of postmodern philosophy that I have elsewhere termed "the ultracritics."[1] For all their differences, they argue that what is claimed as truth is a social construction; what is proposed as universal is historically conditioned. In short, the large-scale rational explanations of Descartes, Locke, Adam Smith, Kant, Hegel, or Marx are not the products of neutral, objective rationality but are inescapably rooted in social and historical contexts. It could be that ultracritics are in the end saying that truth is relative; but it could also be that they are simply unwilling to accept claims that masquerade as universal truth when they are so clearly rooted in context.

On the philosophical level this is a rather sweeping use of a hermeneutic of suspicion. Yet as potent as it seems, it has two flaws that undermine its effectiveness. The first is that, by its nature, ultracriticism has difficulty offering a positive vision of reality. The second is that, insofar as it represents an impulse in the wider culture, it seems to have somewhat undermined Enlightenment rationality while not at all affecting the romanticist alternative.

With regard to rationality, there has been a partial shift in attitudes toward science and instrumental reason. More people are open to alternative explanations of reality—to mystery as well as scientific rationality, and to spirituality as well as naturalism. Moreover, people are more aware of the unintended consequences of scientific research and the lack of moral guidance for at least some of it. Yet if this removes science from its privileged intellectual position, the pervasiveness of science and technology in American culture remains undiminished. Technology, and with it advertising and consumerism, is increasingly shaping our culture and our lives. Renewed openness to spirituality seems not to have diminished either the impact of technology or a lifestyle of consumption. The collapse of universals neither provides moral guidance for our technology nor gives ethical direction to the romanticist expressivism that pervades our culture.

When we focus on religious adherents themselves, the impact of the individualistic market-driven culture is all too evident. In a recent study, sociologist Alan Wolfe reminds us of the classic work of H. Richard Niebuhr, which shows how Christ had transformed culture. But in America, Wolfe concludes: "Culture has transformed Christ, as well as all other religions found within these shores. In every aspect of the religious life, American faith has met American culture—and American culture has triumphed."[2] Whatever churches, denominations, or even persons themselves say they believe, "how we actually live our faith" (Wolfe's subtitle) is highly accommodated to culture.

Evangelicals are no exception to this. Doctrine has strangely disappeared from conservative Protestantism; "impatient with disputation and disagreement," evangelicals have turned away from fundamentalism and are "playing down doctrine in favor of feelings."[3] Committed to sharing their faith and to the necessity of conversion, large numbers of evangelicals nonetheless believe they know too little to answer questions about their faith or are so concerned with avoiding being "unpleasant and ill-mannered" that they are in fact reticent to witness.[4] Embracing the therapeutic culture of modern psychology, evangelicals have replaced language of guilt and accountability to God with nonjudgmental, self-help language. In fact, says Wolfe, "In no area of religious practice, especially for evangelicals, is the gap between the religion as it is supposed to be and religion as it actually is as great as it is in the area of sin."[5]

Wolfe depicts an evangelicalism that acts not so much as an alternative to the culture as it promises to achieve cultural goals more effectively. It is a vehicle for the kind of expressive individualism discussed in the previous chapter. Indeed, the pressure on churches and ministries is to meet the needs of persons who have been shaped not by the gospel but by secular culture.

For his part, Wolfe considers this a largely positive development. Instead of evangelicals and other people of faith anguishing over ways that they "have succumbed to the individualism, and even on occasion the narcissism, of American life," he urges them, "Instead . . . take pride in your flexibility and adaptability." At the same time, he encourages persons concerned about the effect of religious fanaticism on American life not to worry, because most persons of faith "have more in common with you than you realize." Indeed, they "have adapted themselves to modern society far more than you have changed your views about what they are really like."[6] Disagreements over a few social issues should not obscure this deeper commonality.

Not everyone is encouraged by Wolfe's analysis. *Christianity Today* decries the "toothless evangelicalism" Wolfe portrays and calls for us to "nurture an evangelicalism that is truer to its robust heritage." This heritage includes "Bible study that moves beyond personal encouragement to learning about God and his demanding vision for both individuals and society," as well as "an ethic of self-denial" that enables faithfulness.[7] I share this concern. Even Wolfe is not pleased with the "retreat from sin" and the recognition "that covenants exist and that we break them only at great cost to ourselves and to others with whom we share our society."[8] He even has some admiration for fundamentalists who "stand against the emotionality of American culture in favor of ideas—strongly held ideas, to say the least—about who God is and why he asks so much of us."[9]

There is much that could be said about this picture of an emerging postmodern culture. The contrast between doctrinal dispute and an accepting experientialism, or between aggressive evangelism and simply witnessing nonverbally through lifestyle, are the sorts of false choices that the romanticist side of modernity, abetted by a postmodern culture that confuses compassion and tolerance with uncritical affirmation, would foist upon us. I will argue for a theology that seeks to transcend these types of false contrasts and that takes both theology and cultural context with utmost seriousness.

What remains in this section is to underscore the heavy price we pay if we uncritically go with the cultural flow. For that we will look at the work of another sociologist, Robert Wuthnow, on small groups and spirituality in America. While he finds much good in the small group movement, Wuthnow also notes how "they are dramatically changing the way God is understood. God is now less of an external authority and more of an internal presence. The sacred becomes more personal but, in the process, also becomes more manageable, more serviceable in meeting individual needs."[10] Participants in most small groups are encouraged to pray but not to increase in knowledge of Scripture and denominational teachings or to engage in theological reflection. Many small groups "encourage faith to be subjective and pragmatic."[11]

Like Wolfe, Wuthnow argues that small groups are not countering secularity but "*adapting* American religion to the main currents of secular culture." Secularity does not prevent spirituality. Rather, it "encourages a safe, domesticated version of the sacred," a "domesticated deity." Wuthnow states, "From a secular perspective, a divine being is one who is there for our own gratification, like a house

71

pet, rather than one who demands obedience from us, is too powerful or mysterious for us to understand, or who challenges us to a life of service.... People can go about their daily business without having to alter their lives very much."[12] Here again, we see something very much like the individualistic romanticism of modernity continuing to hold us captive. Also again, we see another false contrast, this between a transcendent God and God as an intimate, personal presence.

Wuthnow's research shows clearly what is at stake: will we be set free for a relationship with God as revealed in history or with a God of our own making, and consequently, will we receive and live the new life God offers us through Jesus Christ or settle for trying to enlist God in supporting us in living out our old life? Insofar as we look to postmodern sources for assistance, we will need to look elsewhere than at the ultracritics. But even more, we will need to look at Christian tradition itself for direction in this postmodern culture.

Overcoming the Sacred/Secular Divide

There is a postmodern tendency that offers some hope for reestablishing our relationship with God. Culturally it is manifested as a renewed openness to spirituality and mystery in the face of a world dominated by technology and materialism. Philosophically it takes the form of a suspicion of modern dualism and a preference for holistic or organic depictions of the world. The epistemological dualism of subject/object and the ontological dualism of mind/body have especially been targets of postmodern criticism.[13] I will address anthropological dualisms in a later chapter; here I want to look more carefully at this postmodern embrace of mystery as a means of overcoming another pervasive modern dualism, that between sacred and secular realms.

Although the idea of a secular realm separate and distinct from the sacred is so pervasive in the West today that it seems to be a matter of common sense, in reality it is an invention of Enlightenment modernity. This distinction, which so many of us take for granted, is considered odd by most people on earth and would likewise have seemed odd to most premodern Europeans. It is being increasingly questioned by some in the West today, though often from perspectives and spiritualities that are far from Christian. Yet many modern Christians have resisted this dualism as well, even if they were sometimes forced to use dualistic language to do so. African American Christianity has long offered a more holistic spirituality, as do some elements of Reformed, Wesleyan, and Pentecostal spirituality.

Envisioning a secular realm from which God was effectively removed was seen by modernity as a great advance for human freedom. Prior to the distinction between sacred and secular, God was seen as the hidden cause behind much that occurred, including plagues, wars, earthquakes, floods, and fires. The appropriate human response to these occurrences was repentance for the sins that brought God's judgment, and petition to God to bring a merciful end to the devastation.

The creation of the secular realm opened new possibilities. With God marginalized as a factor, human agency could come to the forefront. Through scientific investigation humanity could understand and perhaps predict natural calamities; through technology humanity could possibly bring them under control or eliminate them entirely. We can cure diseases, detect earthquakes and erect buildings that can withstand them, and build levees to prevent flooding. This is all premised on understanding the causes of these evils as natural. Social science promised an analogous understanding of human psyches and cultures. Again, the hope was that an understanding of the causes of emotional illness, economic crises, and social dysfunction would lead not only to their cure but also to their prevention.

In all of this we find the role of human reason as fundamentally instrumental: its purpose is to exert increasing control over the natural world. This was not only to avert disasters but also to utilize knowledge as a resource for ever-advancing technology. Instrumental reason was the primary tool used to advance human freedom.

There is no question that much of this rational endeavor has been beneficial in alleviating suffering and advancing opportunity. Yet it has its shadow side. As has already been noted, the most evident downside to human technology has been its harm to the environment. But there have been other questionable effects as well. Biological technologies have raised a host of new ethical problems. The same Internet that permits access to an unprecedented amount of information also provides new avenues for child pornography and sexual predation. And technology continues to shape our culture for good or ill, often in unintended ways. In addition to all this, nature has a way of evoking in us a bit more humility about our technological prowess: bacteria become drug resistant; more massive earthquakes bring down our buildings; unprecedented flooding overruns our levees.

As we have seen, romanticism began to criticize Enlightenment rationalism in the late eighteenth century. It emphasized nature rather than technology, and feeling over disengaged reason. Insofar as romanticism addressed the sacred/secular divide at all, it found the sacred within the secular, or better, within nature and the inward self. But the primary focus of the romanticist strand of modernity was not to overcome the sacred/secular divide but the

divide between humanity and nature fostered by instrumental reason.

Liberal theology followed this movement from rationalism to romanticism. The deists of the seventeenth and
eighteenth century embraced Enlightenment rationalism.
They maintained a sharp division between sacred and secular by retaining God as the creator but removing God
from any subsequent involvement in creation, especially
by way of miracles. Rather, they argued that God had con-
structed the world to operate on its own through natural
laws, discoverable by human reason.

The liberals of the nineteenth century were influenced
by romanticism and idealism. They agreed with the deists
that there was no need for God's supernatural, miraculous,
or external intervention in the world, as that would im-
ply creation (and the creator) was somehow deficient. But
instead of a radical removal of God from the world, they
argued that God was an immanent, guiding presence in
history, nature, and human lives—a hidden yet very real
influence lying behind human knowledge and progress.
Thus they opposed the tendency of naturalism and materialism to reject the sacred realm entirely. Their solution
was to overcome the divide by locating the sacred within
the secular.

The desire of liberal theology to maintain the reality of
God against reductionist naturalism and materialism was

commendable. Yet there are at least two problems with the liberal approach. First, it was overly optimistic about human progress, as events in the twentieth century were to demonstrate with horrifying clarity. Given those events, it is questionable what difference God's immanence in history and every human heart actually made. Second, it was overly optimistic about human nature, underemphasizing or denying original sin even as it talked in a variety of ways of God's presence within. Salvation was seen not as a transformation of the heart but as an attunement to the divine presence within. Thus the romanticist tendency to look within ourselves, whether in terms of depth of feeling, moral impulse, or even a heightened rationality, is redescribed from finding that which is our higher nature to finding the divine as well.

The root problem with this approach, as Ludwig Feuerbach recognized, is that God becomes humanity writ large. When we look at history or within ourselves to find God, what we actually find is ourselves. We have in the end Wuthnow's "domesticated deity" and a spirituality far too at home in Western secularity. We may in fact have no deity at all.

It will be a sad irony if theology and the church in the emerging postmodern age, in reaction against instrumental reason and naturalistic reductionism, continues down the romanticist path. There is, fortunately, another path we can take.

The Failure of the Enlightenment Project

In order to discern this alternative path more clearly, we can begin by examining the present state of ethical discourse in the West as seen by Alasdair MacIntyre. Although his focus is on moral theory, his analysis will further clarify why overcoming the sacred/secular dualism requires a different path, as well as clues for what that path might look like.

MacIntyre's concern is the curious way contemporary moral arguments seem to presuppose independent, impersonal premises yet actually rest on rival premises that cannot be weighed against each other.[14] That is, each side appeals to grounds that they seemingly take to be universally accepted but which in fact are not. The result is that there is no way to adjudicate moral debate; each side is left to repeat its position in a louder and more insistent voice. What can account for this predicament?

One plausible answer is emotivism, "the doctrine that all evaluative judgments are *nothing but* expressions of preference, expressions of attitude or feeling, insofar as they are moral or evaluative in character."[15] The impersonal premises to which these judgments appeal are not universal but individual or cultural constructs. The point of evaluative utterance, then, is "the expression of my own feelings or attitudes and the transformation of the feelings and attitudes of others." The purpose of distinctly moral discourse is "the attempt of one will to align the attitudes, feelings, preferences and choices of another with its own."[16] MacIntyre's emotivism is closely linked to what I have been calling the romanticist strand of modernity, or expressive individualism. What is striking about MacIntyre's argument is his claim that, given its origin in the Enlightenment, modern moral discourse had to end in emotivism.

The reason for this is that the "modern self, the emotivist self, in acquiring sovereignty in its own realm lost its traditional boundaries provided by a social identity and a view of human life as ordered to a given end."[17] Premodern moral thought came to be shaped by an Aristotelian structure. Within this "moral scheme" there is "a fundamental contrast between man-as-he-happens-to-be and man-as-he-could-be-if-he-realized-his-essential-nature."[18] That is, the assumption of premodern ethics is that human nature is not as it should be. The purpose of ethics is to describe our essential nature and to prescribe the virtues and practices that enable us to fully become what we in essence are. The structure, then, is teleological; it provides a social identity and moves us toward a given end.

I can put this in more recognizably Christian terms. God created humanity as good, but it has fallen into sin. In redemption God has provided the means to restore humanity and move it toward an eschatological goal. Depictions of the Christian life can be either grounded in creation prior to the fall (in order to restore us to our original nature) or in the eschatological new creation (in order for us to become what we are intended by God to be in the future). Where such depictions cannot be grounded is in humanity as it now is, for it has presently fallen into sin.

Yet this is precisely what the Enlightenment tried to do. By granting authority to human reason and experience it dispensed with that which could not be demonstrated as true on those grounds. Ultimately this meant that any description of human nature resting on a narrative of creation or of new creation was no longer credible.

Enlightenment thinkers, MacIntyre notes, were surprisingly united in seeking to retain the morality they inherited from pre-Enlightenment culture. But unable to appeal to an account of human nature that could not be rationally demonstrated, they sought instead to ground morality in human nature as it is. This is "why the Enlightenment project had to fail," says MacIntyre. "Since the moral injunctions were originally at home in a scheme in which their purpose was to correct, improve and educate human nature, they are clearly not going to be such that they could be deduced from true statements about human nature or justified in some other way by appealing to its characteristics."[19] In other words, the morality they sought to defend cannot be grounded in that which that morality is intended to correct.

The consequence of this failure is that appeal to inherited morality appears arbitrary, "a mere instrument of individual desire and will."[20] To preserve our own moral autonomy we seek to avoid being manipulated by the moral appeals of others; seeking to advance our own convictions we have no alternative than to try to manipulate others through an exercise of power.[21]

Herein lies the postmodern dilemma. Every articulation of a purpose or goal for humanity or the creation is seen as arbitrary and an attempt to exert the power of others (taking away their freedom), but without some account from outside ourselves all we are left with are our own preferences. Should such an account exist—say, a revelation from God—it would be hard under these conditions to recognize it for what it is.

Part III

ENCOUNTERING GOD

Chapter Four

THE PARTICULARITY OF THE PRESENCE OF GOD

As we have seen, a central concern dominating much of Western intellectual history from the Enlightenment to the present is the expansion of human freedom. The hope was that science would liberate people from the age-old depredations of nature and that social science would likewise free them from the limitations of their historical and cultural contexts. People would in an unprecedented way be in charge of their own destinies and be in a position to remake the world.

One perceived threat to this freedom was a God whose laws circumscribed human behavior and dictated human action. Given the common medieval understanding of God, this reaction was understandable. God was depicted as having established a hierarchy of authority and power through both ecclesial and temporal rulers and to question this divine ordering was to challenge the God who had established it. Thus emerged the modern attempt to remove God entirely through atheism, or keep God at a distance through deism, or envision a more supportive deity who reflects our values and affirms our desires but never challenges our inclinations or actions.

But none of that has led to human freedom. Certainly the promise of the Enlightenment has been partially fulfilled. But part of that fulfillment has been to make us aware of how culture continues to hold us captive, sometimes in barely perceptible ways. This cultural captivity includes even those who claim a robust belief in God and the necessity of conversion. We have also seen how a popularized romanticism complicates our dealing with this cultural captivity by encouraging us to identify divinity with our often questionable experiential preferences and inclinations. Moreover, human advances in science and technology, while countering many natural afflictions such as disease, have also enlarged the human capacity to wreak havoc on the environment and on humanity itself through unintended consequences as well as intentional actions. Enlarged human freedom has proved to be an ambiguous gift.

The Enlightenment project failed because it was focused on the human self apart from any account that would give our lives or world purpose and meaning. Because humanity is both finite and compromised by sin, it is unable to ultimately attain genuine freedom. Limited in perspective, humanity lacks the vision to see its dilemma and is therefore subject to cultural captivity. Compromised by sin, it lacks both the capacity and the will to escape it. We must therefore look elsewhere, outside of ourselves, for perspective and power. Our focus must be on God, who sets us free to be the people we were created to be.

But if what has just been claimed is true—that humans are indeed limited by finitude and sin—then our focusing on God is itself a tricky business. We are apt to wrongly conceive of God and end up in idolatry. We will remain trapped within our misperceptions unless God reveals to us who God is and acts to free us from this condition. This is what God has in fact done in Jesus Christ.

My intent in this chapter is to describe more fully the nature of God's revelation and action. In the process I will be making three interrelated claims. First, it is the particular actions of God in the world that reveal who God is (God's identity or otherness). Second, this same God is shown to be present to the world today in such a way that we can enter into a relationship with God. Third, the central forms this presence takes are incarnational and pentecostal.

The Particularity of God

Let me begin by more clearly indicating what I do not mean by the term *God*. There is a pervasive cultural tendency as well as a common philosophical inclination to talk of God by describing the characteristics of deity in general. The assumption is that what we mean by "God" is rooted in some sort of preconceptual experience of divinity, subsequently mediated through human reflection, historical location, and cultural context. Thus in this account the various religions are sometimes thought to have in common an experience and perhaps even a basic concept of divinity but differ as to the secondary characteristics of God. Something like this may well be a common human phenomenon. But I question whether this approach actually enables us to know God. I agree with Colin Gunton that "the weakness of so much modern theology" is that it reduces "the knowledge of God to a speaking *about* ourselves or our supposed experience rather than *from* the God made known in Christ."[1]

But in addition to this, I do not mean the God of classical theism as that God has usually been described. There the tendency has been to begin theological discussions with a conceptual definition of divinity by describing a set of attributes such as omnipotence, omniscience, holiness, and the like. Once these have been established, then it is subsequently asked how divinity so conceived could be triune or become an incarnation. Evangelicals have looked to Scripture for assistance in developing their account of divine attributes, which is certainly the best way to go about it. But even here the assumption that a prior concept of divinity must first be established governs what is selected from Scripture and how it is used theologically.

A number of theologians influenced in varying degrees by Karl Barth have rightly challenged this entire approach. Their central claim is this: in order to know who God is, we need to begin with God's actual revelation in the world. That is, we must focus on the particularity of God's revelation and most especially on the incarnation, cross, and resurrection of Jesus Christ and the coming of the Holy Spirit.

Colin Gunton is an especially insightful proponent of this view. He calls the common attempt to speak of divine "attributes apart from the Trinity...a mistake,"[2] which confuses an abstract description of the characteristics of deity with the identity of the triune God. Gunton's critique is developed through an examination of a wide range of historical theologians. The reason he believes God's actual revelation has been compromised and obscured by the common preference to begin with the divine attributes is because of the dominance of a negative theology that seeks to identify those attributes through concentrating on how God is not like the world. Thus it is said God has power and knowledge but in a way unlike human power and knowledge. God's power and knowledge is therefore fundamentally different from that which we know.

Ostensibly an acknowledgement of theological humility, "negative theology has in effect driven out the positive, so that the God who makes himself known in scripture has been turned into one who cannot be known as he is."[3] As a result, divine attributes are described as timeless qualities apart from God's action in the world. God and the world are conceived in opposition, making it methodologically impossible to think of God's otherness being known by way of God's revelation in the world.[4]

In contrast, Gunton argues it is "the 'descent' of Christ—and all its anticipations in the pages of the Old Testament—who makes God known *in* the world, within the structures of space and time, not *by abstraction from them*."[5] God's being is known through what God has done in creation, salvation, and redemption; "God's actions are *mediated*: he brings about his purposes towards and in the world by the mediating actions of the Son and Spirit."[6] Thus it is the Trinity that identifies God. "We know *who* God is from what he does," and it is this revelation in history that corresponds to God's eternal being.[7]

That we know who God is from God's revelation in history is developed in a different way by Stanley Grenz. He too believes much traditional Christian theology has begun ontologically by connecting the biblical God "with the Greek conception of Being." In Grenz's account, theologians concluded that the revelation of the name of God as I AM (Exod. 3:14), or "I AM WHO I AM," was an ontological claim that meant God "is characterized first and foremost by philosophical traits such as self-existence, eternality, unchangeability, and consequently, absolute being."[8] This long-standing attempt to understand God "on the basis of a prior knowledge of Being"[9] (which Grenz, borrowing from Heidegger, calls "onto-theology"), has met its postmodern demise.

Grenz, like Gunton, proposes to reverse this common approach and ask instead, what are "the implications of the Christian conception of God as triune for…ontology?"[10] He undertakes an extensive exegetical account of the biblical drama of the I AM, from the exodus, exile, and restoration of Israel, through the incarnation of the I AM in Jesus Christ, to "the eschatological sharing of the divine name with the redeemed" through the Spirit.[11] At the heart of this account is the self-naming of the triune God, beginning with the I AM in Exodus and culminating in the interrelation of the three persons of the Trinity. It is through this "ongoing history of relationships" that "the divine name comes to be filled with content."[12]

In developing this trinitarian "theo-ontology" Grenz makes a number of significant observations. First, the drama of the I AM is not about being itself as much as it is about God being present with Israel, and from an eschatological perspective, being present to the entirety of history. Citing Claus Westermann, Grenz declares that divine eternality is not over against history but connected to it.[13] This "dynamic presence" of God "is continuous, constant, and at hand at all times,"[14] and is directly linked to Jesus Christ.

Second, Grenz offers a much more positive role for negative (or apophatic) theology than does Gunton. "Apophatic theology actually provides the very basis for...theo-ontology" in that "it opens the door to revelation and...elevates the category of other as the central feature of reality and, more importantly, even of God."[15] The apophatic warning of the inadequacy of human names for God does not leave God nameless; "the biblical witness is not that the God of the Bible is *un*named, but that God is *self*-named."[16] Thus apophatic theology does not necessarily lead to "complete silence" but rather the "respectful silence" before the transcendent God that opens us to "the speaking of revelation."[17]

Third, apophatic theology also emphasizes otherness. In making this claim Grenz draws upon the apophatic insistence on the radical transcendence of God (God's otherness) to undercut the apophatic emphasis on God as One, beyond even trinitarian language. Grenz argues there is no

God above or beyond the Trinity; oneness and otherness are reciprocally related in God. This means that otherness is eternally present in the triune God, through the persons of the Trinity being other to one another.[18]

Thus, at its best, negative theology reminds us that the goal of theology is not knowledge but love. God ultimately is not found in interiority but in relationship with the other. It is in our love for others that we both image God and "come to know the triune God who is love."[19]

For all of their differences, Grenz and Gunton have a common insistence that to know God's identity we must attend first to the particularity of God's revelation in history. It is *this* God and not some generic "deity" that is the source of our salvation and the model that we are to image. It is *this* God who is definitive of what is meant by freedom, relationality, and love.

The Presence of Transcendence

Grenz's account of the I AM has already addressed my second claim when he speaks of the continual dynamic presence of God. Unfortunately, affirmations of God's presence have been sometimes understood in a way that compromises or even negates the transcendence of God and with it divine otherness and particularity.

David Willis, in his book on the holiness of God, identifies what he calls a three-part "compound mistake":

The first part of the mistake is the tendency to treat transcendence and immanence as opposites (or worse, to speak of the transcendent God versus the immanent God). The second... is the tendency still to think of transcendence and immanence as primarily spatial categories. The third part is the tendency to subsume holiness almost exclusively under God's transcendence.[20]

When the first two parts of this theological mistake are taken together, they produce the misconception that the more transcendent God is, the less God is immanent (or present).

The misconception of transcendence as distance has haunted modern theology. William Placher has shown how transcendence (which meant "otherness" and "mystery" to theologians like Luther and Calvin) was originally understood as complementary to immanence but was reinterpreted by deists and their successors to refer to "distance" in contrast to immanence, which was construed to mean "nearness."[21] Willis insists that "both transcendence and immanence refer to the living Subject who is present but also not restricted to that presence" and that the separateness implied in holy transcendence "refers primarily to uniqueness, not distance from."[22]

So the first point about God's presence is this: the God who is present is the same God whose identity is revealed in all its particularity through God's actions in history. The contemporary agent of that divine presence is the Holy Spirit, and it is through the Spirit that the risen

Jesus Christ is present in both the church and the world. If transcendence refers to otherness, uniqueness, and the like, then what we are speaking of is the presence of transcendence.

To speak of the particularity of the God who is present is not yet to identify the manner of that presence. In the Old Testament, God's presence took a range of forms.[23] There is an omnipresence of God throughout the creation. But there are also occasions when God is intensely, even dangerously present, as on Mount Sinai or in the Holy of Holies. God is also present in yet another way through the anointing of kings and prophets.

The New Testament also depicts diverse modes of divine presence, but two forms of God's presence dominate: the incarnational and the pentecostal.

Incarnational Presence

It is through incarnational presence that God—specifically, the second person of the Trinity—becomes present in space and time as a human being. As John puts it, using his distinctive terminology, "The Word became flesh and lived among us, and we have seen his glory, the glory as of a father's only son, full of grace and truth" (John 1:14). Without ceasing to be the divine Son, in Jesus Christ God has entered into history in a wholly new and unprecedented way. The purpose of incarnational presence is both revelatory and redemptive: through Christ God very concretely reveals the character of God and what it would mean for God's love to reign in the world, and also through Christ "God was pleased to reconcile to himself all things, whether on earth or in heaven, by making peace through the blood of his cross" (Col. 1:20).

We see God's love and reign revealed in Jesus' actions: sins are forgiven, the sick and infirm are healed, demons are cast out, the dead rise, persons of all sorts are treated with dignity, and good news is preached to the poor. We see it as well in Jesus' teachings: to love one another, love our enemies, forgive seventy times seven, minister to "the least of these," and above all to place love for God and seeking God's kingdom at the center of our hearts and our lives.

We see God's redemption in the cross. There, through Jesus Christ, the triune God experiences suffering and death in order that humanity might be reconciled to God, be forgiven of its sins, and receive new life. The barriers between God and humanity—bondage to sin; guilt; shame—are removed, and humanity is enabled to enter into a new relationship with God.

This removal of barriers between humanity and God illumines the distinctive nature of incarnational presence. In Scripture, sin is identified as a central factor in keeping persons from God's presence—from Adam and Eve hiding in the garden to Peter at the lake of Gennesaret saying to Jesus, "Go away from me, Lord, for I am a sinful man!" (Luke 5:8). The forgiveness of sin through redemption on the cross enables reconciliation and a new relationship with God.

However, it is not only sin but also the very power and majesty of God that is a barrier. When God is intensely present, as on Mount Sinai or in the Holy of Holies, people keep their distance. Yet when God is present incarnationally, we find the creator of the universe as a baby in a manger, the God of all glory and majesty as a human being in first-century Palestine. There he was not only accessible; he was vulnerable to suffering and death. When he dies on the cross, the three synoptic Gospels testify that the curtain of the temple separating the people from the Holy of Holies was torn in two (Mark 15:38). Jesus, says Hebrews, is the great high priest who can "sympathize with our weaknesses" because he "has been tested as we are, yet without sin. Let us therefore approach the throne of grace with boldness, so that we may receive mercy and find grace to help in time of need" (Heb. 4:15-16). What Jesus' life and death made possible was a new relationship with God, modeled on the relationship of Jesus to the Father, in which persons can not only approach God but also interact with God. It enables a kind of intimacy with God without diminishing God's transcendence or majesty.

Indeed, it is in the cross that we come to know the height and depth of God's majesty as well as God's love.

Jesus' death on the cross is inextricably connected to his life. On one level, it is his teachings and actions that motivate others to put him to death. From their perspective, his death is the repudiation of the life he led and the denial of his being revelatory of God. But on another level, Jesus' death on a cross is God's plan to redeem the humanity God loves while at the same time judging the sin that is destructive of both our relationship with God and of human and nonhuman creation. From this perspective it is precisely for this purpose that God is present in Jesus Christ. This means the cross is not only redemptive but also revelatory: "God proves his love for us in that while we still were sinners Christ died for us" (Rom. 5:8).

Were Jesus not risen from the dead, we would not be speaking of incarnational presence or the redemptive power of the cross. Without the Resurrection the cross would represent one more tragic death, one more profoundly good life brought to an untimely end by forces too powerful to overcome. But because Jesus is risen and alive, *this* Jesus—the one who lived as he did and died as he did—is both Lord and Savior. Sin and death are overcome and principalities and powers are overthrown. It is through his death that we have life, and it is the life he embodied and now gives to us that is eternal. The love manifested in his life and in his death on a cross is not sealed in a tomb but lives and reigns and ultimately will renew all creation when Jesus comes again. And in this time between Easter and that second coming, we have the assurance that "neither death, nor life, nor angels, nor rulers, nor things present, nor things to come, nor powers, nor height, nor depth, nor anything else in all creation, will be able to separate us from the love of God in Christ Jesus our Lord" (Rom. 8:38-39).

This then is how God is present incarnationally in Jesus Christ.[24] God is revealed in a particular human life, within a particular culture, and at a particular point in history. It is through the life, death, and resurrection of this Jesus that humanity has salvation, and it is this same Jesus who reigns as Lord and is coming again to transform all of creation in love. There is no way to properly identify the character and nature of God that does not make Jesus Christ definitive and ultimate.

Pentecostal Presence

It is through pentecostal presence that God—specifically, the third person of the Trinity—is present in power throughout the world. In the Incarnation, God was present by becoming human, and thereby also was limited, as humans are, to a particular time in history and a particular culture and geographic space. In contrast, pentecostal presence is universal: God is present in all times and places. One does not have to live in first-century Palestine to encounter the presence of God.

It is important at the outset to state that the God who is universally present is none other than the God revealed in Jesus Christ. Pentecostal presence neither supplants nor separately coexists with incarnational presence. God is still definitively known in Jesus Christ. Pentecostal presence enables everyone in all times and places to know and be transformed by this God. In like manner, pentecostal presence does not provide a separate and complementary redemption to that accomplished by Jesus' death and resurrection. Rather, it enables persons to trust in Christ, experience forgiveness, be reconciled to God, and receive and grow in a new life of love, all on the basis of what Christ has accomplished.

The focus of pentecostal presence, then, is the actual salvation of persons, understood both as justification and sanctification, as well as the empowerment of persons to enable their participation in the mission of God in the world. Put differently, the Holy Spirit creates a church whose focus is on the worship of God, whose life together reflects that of the kingdom of God, and whose motivation and outreach are intrinsically missional.

It is important to note that the universal character of pentecostal presence does not entail a loss of sovereignty on the part of God. The Spirit still "blows where it chooses" (John 3:8), still decides to show or hide that presence. To say salvation is universally available or the Spirit is universally present is not to say we can access the Spirit whenever we want for whatever purposes we want.[25]

This work of the Spirit can be further illuminated by comparison with incarnational presence. In becoming incarnate, the Son did not cease to be divine, retaining all authority and glory (however hidden) as well as all that characterizes God, most especially love. Yet as the hymn in Philippians 2 implies, in becoming human there was a voluntary self-emptying, a laying aside of divine power in order to take on humanity with all its vulnerability and limitations. Thus "he humbled himself / and became obedient to the point of death— / even death on a cross" (Phil. 2:8). That is, without ceasing to be the divine Son, he became capable of genuine human obedience to God and to the reality of death itself.

But it also opens Jesus to another human reality—the presence and power of the Holy Spirit. Jesus was baptized by the Spirit, led by the Spirit, and empowered by the Spirit. As both John and Luke make clear, this same guidance and empowerment is available for all who follow Jesus. In John, the Spirit is "another paraclete" (like Jesus) who will abide with the disciples, reminding them of Jesus' teachings (John 14:26). In Luke/Acts the Holy

Spirit who fills the disciples on the day of Pentecost is the same Holy Spirit who had baptized Jesus and who in Acts enables the disciples to say and do the sorts of things Jesus said and did.

Yet the differences between the disciples and Jesus are more significant than the similarities. The disciples are not divine; they have no authority and glory of their own. Their authority for both teaching and miracles is Jesus Christ, in whose name they speak and act, and it is to him they give glory. Their lives and their deaths do not redeem others but witness to the One whose death does provide redemption. Although they have received the Spirit, it is only Jesus who is given Spirit without measure. Finally, as sinners, they do not have divine love at the core of their being from the beginning; rather, the Spirit, on the basis of Christ's death and resurrection, gives them a new life of love.

Pentecostal presence, then, enables and invites persons to trust in Christ for their salvation and enter into a transforming relationship with Christ through the Spirit. This transformation of the heart and life occurs in response to what God has done in Christ and then enables imitation of Christ's words and acts. Pentecostal presence builds communities centered on worship of God and love for one another and leads and empowers those communities to participate in God's mission in the world.

It is the presence of God in these incarnational and pentecostal forms that provides for true human freedom. Such freedom is neither intrinsic to human nature nor attainable through human reason or experience. It is, instead, a gift of God through the particular life, death, and resurrection of Jesus Christ. Because God's nature and redemption is necessarily defined by the particularity of Christ, the Christian life is necessarily particular as well. The freedom it is given is most fundamentally the freedom to love God, others, and creation in the same way that God has loved us in Christ.

Chapter Five

THE TRANSFORMATION OF THE HEART

What does it mean to say we have a new heart or are living a new life? Evangelicals speak the language of conversion, new birth, and regeneration to denote an inward transformation of the heart by God that decisively changes how we live. But to say *that* it happens is not the same as saying *what* happens or *how* it happens, much less what difference it makes. Although others have certainly addressed these matters, sometimes in an especially comprehensive fashion,[1] I want to focus on three critical aspects of the transformation of the heart. First, what constitutes a changed heart and makes it distinctly Christian? Second, how does such a conversion occur? And third, what difference does it make for how we live out the new life we have received? Foundational to these goals is the recovery of the language of the affections.

The Recovery of the Affections

Jonathan Edwards, writing during the eighteenth-century awakening that gave birth to evangelicalism, argued that "true religion, in great part, consists in holy affections."[2] John Wesley, who abridged and published Edwards's *Treatise Concerning Religious Affections* in England, made a similar claim: "True religion, the very essence of it, is nothing short of holy tempers."[3]

In Wesley's theology, "affections" and "tempers" are related terms; some would argue they are synonyms.[4] For our purposes it is enough to note that both Edwards and Wesley used such terms to describe the content of a heart transformed by God and of lives growing in sanctification. If not equivalent to the Pauline term "fruit of the Spirit," affections and tempers certainly include those aspects of Christian character that are the most central, including faith, hope, and love.

In Edwards and Wesley, affections and tempers are identical to the disposition or inclination of the will. Thus to change our affections is to change our wills. For the Calvinist Edwards, the bondage of our will to sin is broken by the new birth, in which the Holy Spirit creates in us holy affections. For the Arminian Wesley, the Holy Spirit has already been at work preveniently, graciously restoring our liberty such that we can resist the inclination of our will. Nonetheless, he agrees that the power of sin over our will is broken with the new birth through the Holy Spirit giving us holy tempers. The new birth, then, is the inception of new dispositions in the heart, which then grow and strengthen through sanctification.

This understanding of affections or tempers was effectively lost in nineteenth-century Calvinism and Wesleyanism. What replaced it was an anthropology derived from Enlightenment philosophy that envisions the will as caught between a conflict between reason and emotions. Rationalists thought our higher capacity of reason should control the will over our lower, sinful emotions. Romanticists believed our more natural emotional nature should direct the will rather than a somewhat artificial rationality. American evangelicals tended toward the rationalist view, but advocates of both had lost the more holistic anthropology of Edwards and Wesley.

Two developments in the second half of the twentieth century laid the groundwork for a recovery of the affections and tempers in contemporary theology. The first was the recovery of virtue or character ethics, initiated by Alasdair McIntyre's *After Virtue* in 1981.[5] A host of writers began to develop this form of ethical reflection, including the prolific Stanley Hauerwas and the evangelical theologian Jonathan Wilson.[6]

Virtue ethics has an ancient lineage going back to Greek philosophy and patristic Christianity and was further developed by medieval theologians such as Thomas Aquinas. In contrast to more modern forms of ethics that ask what we should *do* (and thus focus on ethical dilemmas), virtue ethics asks what sort of person we should *be* (and how we can attain that character). Virtues are those habitual inclinations that both enable and predispose us to act in certain ways. If we are honest and compassionate, then we will tend to act in an honest and compassionate manner.

We acquire and develop virtues through practicing them within a particular community. The community is itself shaped by an overarching story or narrative that enables the community to identify the ethical common good as well as the virtues needed to move toward it. For Christians, the story of God as revealed in history and Scripture identifies what is good and the virtues necessary to live our lives accordingly. The virtues are acquired and strengthened through Christian practices or disciplines, such as worship, a devotional life, communal interaction, and service to others.

Along with the resurgence of interest in virtue ethics,

a second development in the 1980s was foundational for the contemporary recovery of affections and tempers. This was the new focus on emotions in moral philosophy, most notably by Robert C. Solomon, Martha C. Nussbaum, and Robert C. Roberts.[7] Their work interacts with a wider discussion on the nature of emotion involving philosophers, historians, psychologists, biologists, anthropologists, and sociologists. In his book *The Passions*, first published in 1976, Solomon argues against the reason-versus-passions myth,[8] instead proposing that "the emotions are themselves rational (and therefore sometimes irrational too), ...ways of seeing and engaging in the world."[9] Both he and Nussbaum understand emotions to be judgments— that is, they are forms of evaluation or appraisal of, or assent to, how the world seems to us. For Roberts most emotions are better described as "concern-based construals," ways of seeing and experiencing the world "imbued, flavored, colored, drenched, suffused, laden, informed, or permeated with concern."[10] Of course, judgments or construals can be inexact or incorrect but the rationality of emotions is not negated by that fact.

It is the confluence of virtues ethics and the understanding of emotions as judgments or construals that has made the recovery of the language of affections and tempers so persuasive and appealing. Affections (to use that term to encompass as well the meaning of tempers for

Wesley) are like emotions as described by the moral philosophers and virtues as described by the ethicists. Yet they have the additional advantage of making clear their inception and development through transforming experiences with God. Two theologians in particular have provided sustained accounts of something akin to the affections.

Robert C. Roberts, as we have seen, understands most emotions to be concern-based construals. By "construal" he means an "interpretative perception," a way of understanding our world or situation in it. As interpretations, "emotions can be right or wrong about the situation." Because they are concern-based they also involve our being affected in some way by the construal—that is, the situation as we construe it is related to something we care about. The emotion—be it fear, compassion, hope, or the like—is the result of the construal related to the concern. Differing construals or differing concerns produce different emotions.[11] Hence Roberts defines a concern as an "emotion-disposition"—that is, the disposition to have certain emotions depending on how we construe a situation.[12]

In mature persons some concerns are orienting in that they "integrate and focus the personality and give a person 'character.'" Roberts calls this orienting concern a "passion." Here Roberts draws on one of the several meanings of passion, namely "a person's long-term, *characteristic* interests, concerns, and preoccupations."[13] Thus he is not thinking of passion as intensity of feeling but as having a passion for something. Christians have a passion for the gospel and the kingdom of God.[14]

What makes the Christian life distinct is that Christian concepts and narratives shape it. "Each of the Christian emotions is a construal of the subject's situation"—both in the immediate and larger context—in terms of the gospel and the kingdom of God, and "incorporate elements of basic Christian doctrine."[15] Thus "Christian joy is joy in the Lord, gratitude is gratitude to God for his grace in Jesus Christ…and so forth."[16] A mature Christian is one whose heart has been shaped by Christian teachings and is thereby disposed to actions "characteristic of the kingdom of God."[17]

For Roberts, emotions are one category of virtues.[18] As construals, emotions combine elements of passive receptivity and voluntary control. Sometimes they happen to us as we construe a situation, but often we can alter our emotions by acting as if we see things differently. To begin to worship and serve along with Christians could be the doorway to looking at the world in Christian terms and eventually coming to believe what Christians believe.[19]

Among the many valuable insights that can be derived from Roberts's account is one directly related to the issue raised in chapter 2: if conversion is transformational, why do Christians so converted remain oblivious to systemic racism or uncritically immersed in consumerism? We will later argue, using Roberts's terms, that while they may have received and are growing in Christian emotion-dispositions, they are at the same time misconstruing their more immediate context. They are thus disposed to Christian emotions but actually lack them in certain instances because of those errors of construal.

The second theologian to provide a contemporary account of the affections is Don E. Saliers. Because the word *emotion* is loosely used to cover a wide range of phenomena such as feelings and moods, Saliers reclaims the term *affection* to designate "a basic attunement which lies at the heart of a person's way of being and acting."[20] Affections "are necessarily tied to how we describe and assess the world"; so, for example, to have compassion for human suffering is to see the world differently from someone who does not have that compassion.[21]

Christian affections are shaped over time by the narratives, teaching, and practice of the Christian faith, which are the means through which we come to know God and the world. Thus, "the language of prayer...evokes and educates us in certain specific emotions by ascribing to God what is believed about God, in the vocative mode."[22] Thus worship and prayer not only express emotion but critique it as well.

The affections are not only expressions of the Christian life but also learned capacities that dwell in the heart. Affections are more who we *are* than what we *feel*; they are core aspects of our character.[23] Affections, then, may give rise to feelings but are not themselves feelings. They are dispositions to act and feel, the "motives and wellsprings of desire and action" in the heart.[24]

Saliers's account in many ways overlaps that of Roberts. He too offers important clues to the possibilities and limits of conversion. The nature of an affection is fundamentally what it is because of its object. To love God, then, is given content through what we believe about God and how we have experienced God. Impoverished practices of worship, prayer, community, and service limit our belief and experience and thereby can make conversion transformative yet inadequate. Although we can always grow in the knowledge and love of God, our growth is in part dependent on participation in a community whose worship and service are as deep and rich as the gospel of Jesus Christ.

The Nature of the Affections

Having briefly discussed the recovery of the language of affections (or emotion-dispositions) as most centrally constituting the heart, I now want to provide a more analytical sketch of their central characteristics, highlighting especially what it means for an affection to be "Christian."

We can begin by noting that affections are intrinsically *relational*—that is, they are always directed toward an object. We do not, for example, simply "love"; we always love someone or something. Christians love God as revealed in Jesus Christ, and their neighbor as themselves.

Christian affections are relational in another sense as well. They are evoked and nurtured in response to God's actions and promises in Christ, through the presence and power of the Holy Spirit in our lives. Thus relationship here is not simply being directed toward an object, for this Object is a living, active Subject whom we came to know and experience. This is a fundamentally transforming relationship.

There are three important implications of the relationality of the affections. First, although we *have* affections as traits of Christian character, we cannot possess them apart from God. They are who we are and give us a Christian identity only insofar as we are in an ongoing relationship with God. This means our having affections provides no grounds for claiming inherent righteousness apart from God: salvation remains "by grace alone." As John Wesley said, "Christ does not give life to the soul separate from, but in and with himself."[25]

This means, second, that our character is itself constituted by relationship. In contrast to Enlightenment modernity's assumption that each person is a self-subsisting, autonomous individual, the logic of the affections is in harmony with the postmodern observation that persons are actually the product of the complex web of relationships within which they live. This is not deterministic, as persons have agency and act on their relational environment as well as being shaped by it. Christian affections govern the lives of those persons who have experienced the transforming love of God in Christ and have had their lives reordered accordingly.

A third implication of the relationality of the affections is that it provides a way of addressing a conundrum in Wesleyan holiness theology—that is, whether the change that occurs in sanctification is substantive or relational. If one assumes an anthropology of autonomous individualism, then to understand sanctification as relational is inherently weak; for if relationships are essentially external to the self, it would leave the self unchanged. To many in the Wesleyan holiness tradition this sounds Calvinistic, changing outward behavior while accepting that sin will always rule the heart. But if who we are is constituted by our relationships, then to change the relationship *is* to change the self. A relationship with God will change us at the very core of our being. This was something understood not only by Wesley but also by the very Calvinist Edwards as well.

Affections, then, are not simply relational; they are also *shaped by their object*. The object of the affection determines the nature of the affection. For example, to love God as revealed in Jesus Christ is manifested through a range of attitudes and actions such as thanksgiving, praise, obedience, and service. Love for our neighbor is expressed through such things as compassion, hospitality, and self-giving. An unholy affection such as love for money would be manifested by greed, self-centeredness, manipulation of others, and the like. Notice that while the word *love* is used in each of these three examples, what it means concretely to love varies according to its object. Thus the object of an affection leads to distinctive attitudes, values, actions, and ways of relating to others and to creation. Affections in the heart produce corresponding ways of living.

The concreteness of this shaping of affections by their object should be underscored. We have already seen the particularity of God's revelation in Jesus Christ. Because the affections are in response to and shaped by that revelation, the affections reflect the particularity of God. That means that to love God is not an expression of some universal human characteristic but is constituted by what it means to love *this* God, who was incarnate in Jesus Christ, living and teaching and then dying out of love for us on a cross. Likewise, to love one's neighbor is not to have some generalized good feeling for others but to have the same love for our neighbor that God has for us in Christ and to identify our neighbor in the same way that Christ did. Because Jesus Christ is alive and coming again to fully transform creation, to have and to grow in these affections is to already live as members of the eschatological kingdom of God.

Because affections are directed toward objects, and in many cases are also responses to those objects, they are *dispositions* of the heart. When they take root in our lives, they become the inclinations and desires that make us the persons we are. Affections are emotions, but they are not "feelings" as that term is commonly understood. Feelings are transitory; they come and go. Affections are deeper, enduring traits of character that give us the capacity to have certain feelings. Thus to *be* a compassionate person is in part to have the capacity to *feel* compassion, and to be a hopeful person is what enables one to *have* hope. But as we have already seen, more concretely we are persons who are compassionate and hopeful with respect to certain objects (compassionate for our neighbor as defined by Jesus' teaching, hopeful in God's promises, and so on), and this means our feelings will be produced in situations that influence these particular objects of our affections (or in Roberts's language, our concerns).

As dispositions, affections not only incline us to have certain feelings, they also motivate us for action. If we are compassionate for our neighbor and encounter a situation that elicits our compassionate concern, we also have an inclination to take some action on our neighbor's behalf. We may or may not actually take action—there may be countervailing circumstances that impede action, or a lack of opportunity, or no clear way to act beneficially—but whether we act or not, the motivation to do so is there because of the presence of the affection. And, because they motivate us, they also serve as *reasons* for our actions: the reason we went to the aid of the hurricane victims is because we had compassion for them.

This leads to one further characteristic of the affections: they are *ways of seeing*, lenses through which we perceive and interpret our world. A compassionate person sees and understands the world quite differently from someone who lacks compassion. Christian affections, then, should enable us to gradually see the world as God sees it and to love the world as God loves it. They should enable us to envision what it might mean for God's will to be done on earth as it is in heaven and thereby participate in God's mission in the world. This capacity to increasingly see with new eyes does not mean we easily and naturally come to see everything with clarity, however; as we have seen, deep-rooted cultural assumptions that are actually contrary to God's reign and love can seem normal and obvious. Nonetheless, Christian affections do provide an inclination and desire to see things as God sees them, as well as an openness to new perspectives.

One important implication of understanding the Christian life as essentially having affections is this distinction: the new life in Christ is first of all about the transformation of the heart by the Holy Spirit in response to what God has done for us in Jesus Christ; it is secondarily and as a result of this transformation our following or imitating Christ. In part this is simply saying that we love because God first loved us (see 1 John 4:19). That is, our experience of God's love in Christ transforms the heart, and it is the resulting affections that give us the dispositions and vision to then love as Jesus Christ loves. To emulate Christ's actions or obey Christ's teachings we must be the kind of people who would desire to do that, and we become that sort of people by responding to what God has done for us in Christ's death and resurrection. This distinction should not be overdrawn: it is also the case that awakened sinners and serious seekers, through trying to follow Christ, can come to experience a transformation of the heart. When they do, they will then find a new desire to follow Jesus springing up within them, one now grounded in knowing God's love and in gratitude for that love in Jesus Christ.

The Nature of Conversion

How, then, does this transformation of the heart occur? The short answer is through conversion, a gracious work of the Holy Spirit. Because it is an act of God, we should not be too quick to prescribe a specific set of events or experiences that must occur, or insist on their arrangement in a fixed sequence. Gordon T. Smith, for example, has identified a cluster of seven elements in Scripture that together constitute a holistic conversion but wisely avoids placing them in a necessary sequence or insisting that they occur in a particular way.[26]

Yet allowing for this diversity, conversion does have a logical shape. Conversion necessarily implies change—moving from one set of dispositions to another, one set of beliefs to another, one way of life to another, one governing passion to another. The call for conversion presupposes a need for conversion. Conversion is discontinuous; it argues that what is needed is not to go deeper into ourselves but to encounter the living God who is other than ourselves. What we need is not self-discovery but transformation. This does not mean that God is not already at work within us. It means that the God who works within us does so without losing God's transcendent otherness and awakens in us a holy discontent with the shape and direction of our lives. The effect of this prevenient grace is more convicting than affirming; it seeks to break us out of our illusion of self-sufficiency and enable us to recognize our real need.

Two theologians who are especially helpful in developing an understanding of conversion compatible with the approach I am taking here are George W. Stroup and

Cheryl Bridges Johns. Stroup centers his discussion on the role of narrative; Johns focuses hers on the affections.

Stroup describes conversion as precipitated by a "collision of narratives," when "the narrative identity of an individual collides with the narrative identity of the Christian community" and the revelation of God is thereby experienced.[27] This collision creates the possibility that the one who has encountered "the Christian community with its narratives, common life, and faith claims about reality" will then "begin the lengthy process of reinterpreting his or her personal history in light of the narratives and symbols that give the Christian community its identity."[28]

This encounter can occur to persons who are outside the community or to those who have spent their lives in the church but have yet to appropriate the Christian faith and understand themselves in terms of it. Of course, some will reject the new narrative in favor of maintaining their preexisting identity and others may seek to modify their previous self-understanding in light of it. But those undergoing conversion "experience significant disorientation, a sense that the world as they know it is coming apart, that their understanding of reality no longer quite coheres with their experience."[29] It is at the point where narratives collide that faith can be born, "that identities, even worlds, may be altered and reality perceived in a radically new way."[30]

In Stroup's account the revelation of God in Jesus Christ is encountered as a narrative that calls into question understandings of self and reality. To those who trust in Jesus Christ it promises and enables a new understanding of self and the world and consequently a new identity and way of life.

Cheryl Bridges Johns draws upon the earlier work of James E. Loder,[31] modifying his five steps in terms of a more Wesleyan and pentecostal theology of transformation and the affections. The first step, *conflict*, "occurs in the dissonance between that which is and that which should be." The cause of our present condition is a brokenness of creation and humanity that "results in a distortion of reality and misguided affections." The dissonance reveals not only our condition but also our inability to repair the damage.[32] It underscores our need for grace.

This begins the *scanning process* in which we actively seek solutions to the problem revealed by the conflict. At the same time, the Holy Spirit is at work, seeking to guide our search and draw us to God. Some may at this time begin participating in the life and practices of a Christian community. In John Wesley's language, this is akin to being awakened and under conviction, and having what he called "the faith of a servant." Johns notes that the most difficult part of this process "is the need to wait, to tarry awhile in the conflict." Although tempted to seek "premature closure," it is as we wait that we already begin to grow in grace and are drawn ever closer to God.[33]

The culmination of this process is *interruptive insight by transforming Presence.* This heals the rupture in our understanding of the world, brings new meaning out of the conflict, and creatively gives new "birth to the imagination." This in turn brings *release and mundane ecstasy* in which the "beauty of holiness is revealed and our hearts are realigned toward the object of our affections. This movement is characterized by testimony and worship."[34] For Wesley, this is regeneration, or the new birth. In the final stage, "we experience the *verification* of God's transforming power."[35] This, Wesley would call "assurance," the witness of the Spirit. Johns says it enables us to newly see how God has been working in our lives as well as look forward to our growth in love for God and neighbor in the future.

What Johns contributes is to provide a description of conversion from the standpoint of the one undergoing it. Whereas it is rightly depicted as a process, it is a process initiated by a crisis, a conflict between *is* and *ought* that only God can resolve by a transformation of the understanding and the affections.

If we can now draw these two proposals together with what has been previously said about God's revelation and the affections of the heart, something like the following picture of conversion emerges. First, we live in a fallen world, and our affections and beliefs reflect that world. We desire those things our culture has identified as good and understand our lives and the world in terms of its depiction of normality. This means our lives are governed by unholy affections, some on account of having inappropriate objects and others whose objects are appropriate in themselves but have taken on disproportionate significance, supplanting the centrality of God.

Second, the Holy Spirit is at work cultivating a sense of unease concerning our lives and our world. While in one sense the way things are seems both natural and normal, there is the countervailing sense that all is not as it should be. Things are not all right with the world, nor are we living as we should. We do not perhaps understand the fullness of the problem, but we do have a sense that there *is* a problem.

Third, this conflict between *is* and *ought* is clarified and intensified by an encounter with the message and promise of the gospel. Whether by proclamation, testimony, worship, devotional reading, or the like, there is now a diagnosis of our condition and the promise of its healing through Christ. It is here that our preexisting "narrative" and identity collides with the gospel narrative and we have to decide whether to hold on to the old or seek to embrace the new through trusting in what God has done in Jesus Christ. This trusting, or faith, is more something we desire than a product of our will. Our faith itself is a gift we receive from God, perhaps, as Johns says, after much tarrying, but always with a receptive heart. It may come to us with perceptible suddenness or we may more gradually become aware that we have begun to trust in Christ. But either way, this trust in Christ begins a lifelong process of reinterpreting our lives and the world in terms of the gospel narrative, and living accordingly.[36]

Conversion, then, is a work of God in the heart and the life. It brings with it new understanding, new relationships, and new affections. In terms of understanding, conversion brings, in the words of Helmut Thielicke, the "death of the old Cartesian self."[37] The gospel is not something we can incorporate into our preexisting understanding; it reconstructs our understanding of the world and of ourselves. Instead of interpreting things from our perspective, we begin to interpret things from God's perspective. The ground for this new understanding is the resurrection of Jesus Christ, which not only is the first fruits of the age to come but also precipitates a paradigm shift in which old ways of thinking must be rejected or reinterpreted in light of the new.[38]

It brings new relationships through the atonement of Jesus Christ. Because we experience forgiveness of our sins through the cross of Christ (justification), our relationship with God is fundamentally altered. Rather than avoiding

God or simply dutifully seeking to obey God, our hearts and lives are now responding to God's gracious love in Christ. We are now free to love both God and neighbor—not to obtain acceptance but because we have been accepted.

This transformation of our relationship with God enables the transformation of the heart. The God revealed in Jesus Christ is now the object of our governing affection, and close by it are love for our neighbor and for God's creation. And as our affections are changed, so is our life. We begin living differently because we *are* different.

Conversion does not of course change everything at once. We grow in our affections and our understanding (sanctification) as we grow in the knowledge and love of God and of our neighbor and world. But conversion does lay a new foundation in the heart, awaken a new set of desires and motivations, and give life new meaning and direction.

Part IV

FREEDOM TO LOVE

Chapter Six

SET FREE TO LOVE

In salvation God sets us free from sin by giving us a new life, motivated and governed by love. Through salvation we are set free to be the people we were created to be, people in the image of God who *is* love.

But this freedom does not come automatically. The new foundation that conversion lays in the heart sits uneasily beside an older set of sinful dispositions and understandings, often given to us by our culture. The popular romanticism embedded in social practices and inculcated by media continues to draw us away from the freedom God gives, to a captivity that masquerades as freedom. How, then, are these new affections or tempers retained and nurtured while we live in a world that has a very different sense of what is normal and natural? How do we live *in* the world as ones not *of* the world?

There are really two interrelated problems here, one "internal" and the other "external." The internal problem has to do with what John Wesley called "holiness of heart": how do we retain and nurture the holy affections or tempers given in new birth, which gives us the motivation and desire to love God, love our neighbor, and care for God's creation? That will be the focus of this chapter. The external problem has to do with what Wesley called "holiness of life": how do we faithfully and effectively live out these motivations and desires in a culture that keeps us from seeing or understanding the world as God sees it? That will be the subject of chapter 7.

Obstacles to Holy Affections

The conversion of the heart evokes new dispositions centered on a love for God and neighbor. There is now a desire for God and motivation to participate in redemptive mission in the world. There is the dawning of a new understanding of the meaning and purpose of life. But as we have just said, this is a beginning. These new affections must take root and grow if the Christian life is to be sustained over time and salvation is to bring us to the goal of recovering the image of God in fullness.

The obstacles to this growth in love and other Christian affections are formidable. In the eighteenth century John Wesley identified three categories of desire that compete for our allegiance. There are the "desires of the flesh," those things that give pleasure through taste, smell, or touch. There are "desires of the eye," which please the imagination through sight or hearing. And there is "the pride of life," which are those things that gain status in the eyes of the world, evoking the praise and esteem of others.[1] Some of these things are not evil in themselves—we can enjoy the pleasures of nature or art, for example. But even these become evil when they become the center of our desiring, governing our hearts and lives in place of God.

These desires are pervasive in the twenty-first century, inculcated by advertising, the entertainment media, and the practices of everyday living. Much of this is so normal to American life that to object seems odd or unnecessarily extreme.

To take only one example, Philip D. Kenneson provides an astute analysis of the impact of the market economy on the Christian life. While readily acknowledging its great strength in productivity and efficiency, Kenneson shows how our everyday participation in the practices of the market shapes our hearts and lives in ways contrary to God.

Central to its detrimental effect is its promotion of self-interest. Although the market "*could* be viewed as a mechanism for rendering mutual service," it actually encourages us to view our relations with one another primarily to enhance our existence and material well-being. We therefore tend to see others "as actors in *our* drama... [where] these people play the part of producers of goods and services for *us,* or of potential customers for *our* goods and services, or of competitors whose own attempts to secure their livelihood may threaten *our* attempt to do the same."[2] How, asks Kenneson, can we be directed toward others the way love requires when so much of what we actually do in life encourages us to "pay attention to others only to the extent that they can benefit us"?[3]

A second detrimental effect on the Christian life is on how we evaluate human worth and dignity. Because the market values the skills and abilities of persons in the same way it does goods and services, it is only natural for us to assume that wealth and income indicate relative human worth. We are then led to value certain occupations and persons more highly than others. Work that is paid little (such as menial labor) or nothing at all (such as that of a stay-at-home parent) is devalued, along with the persons who do it. What is worse is that the persons in those jobs often devalue themselves.[4]

How different this is from how God evaluates persons—God who not only created everyone in the divine image but who also through the Incarnation undergoes death on a cross out of love for all. How different this is from the life and teaching of Jesus, who treated women, children, lepers, the poor—indeed everyone who was on the margins of society—as persons of worth and dignity.

Furthermore, as Kenneson notes, market perspectives often find a home in the life of the church. His example is the all-too-common practice of a local church seeking to attract members through programs designed to appeal to their self-interest.[5] In this way the church (and the gospel) becomes one more consumer choice, rather than an invitation to an alternative way of life to that of consumerism.

In fact, there are a multitude of ways the perspectives and practices of the market can and have shaped the life of the church. The survival and enhancement of a local church or a denomination can become the lens though which ministry is planned and assessed. Worship can be evaluated in terms of whether participants feel they have gotten something out of it. Evangelism practices can be judged on numbers alone. The worth and stature of churches can be assessed in terms of membership and budgets, and that of pastors by income and public prominence.

The culture of the market evokes and shapes very different affections from those of the gospel. The desires and motivations it nurtures, its construal of the world, its implicit narrative of the meaning and purpose of life all run counter to the new life given by God through Jesus Christ.

If we are to remain and grow in love and other fruit of the Spirit, how do we do so in the face of this and other powerful cultural influences that can so deeply shape our hearts and lives?

Growing in the Knowledge and Love of God

We can begin to answer this question by drawing an analogy with how we know other persons. When we meet others, they are present to us, whether physically or through communications media. But in addition to our having contact with them, what is evident from the beginning is their distinctiveness—no one else is exactly like them. Each has his or her own personality and story, character and perspectives. If we continue a relationship with them over time, we will come to know them in all their particularity more fully and deeply.

A relationship with God is much like this. We can encounter God because God is universally present and accessible to us through the Holy Spirit (what we earlier called pentecostal presence). And the God who is present is none other than the God who is revealed in Jesus Christ (incarnational presence). God thus has a distinctive character and story.

Of course, an encounter with God is qualitatively different from meeting another person, however striking or significant. Encountering God is potentially transformative in a life-changing way. To recall George W. Stroup's imagery, it involves a collision of narratives in which God's story of creation and redemption through Jesus Christ invites a radical reinterpretation of the meaning and purpose of our lives and world. With that reinterpretation comes a changed heart and the birth of new dispositions, motivations, and desires.

But where the analogy holds is this: we come to know God more fully and deeply as we continue to be in relationship with God over time. And because it is a relationship with *God*, it is intrinsically transformative in that we grow in our love for God and neighbor as well as all accompanying fruit of the Spirit.

One important aspect of any human relationship is our embodiment. That is, it is in and through our bodies that we speak and enact our intentions and thereby display our character. It is through our embodied actions, both past and present, that others come to know who we are. Of course, we can misinterpret another's speech or actions and come to have false beliefs about the person. But the only avenue for correcting those beliefs is a fresh consideration of the person's embodied speech and actions over time.

Because God's presence is spiritual, it is not embodied. This is not to say that God does not have personal agency or cannot enact intentions[6] but that we cannot know God in the embodied manner that we know another person. As I have argued elsewhere, our knowledge of God is therefore necessarily grounded in Scripture, which through narrative and other genres provides a descriptive account of God's intentions and actions in creation and history, including God's own incarnational embodiment in Jesus Christ.[7] Thus God's character is revealed in narratives through God's interaction with circumstances; in the prophets through God's admonition and promise; in psalms through the assumptions underlying their praise, thanksgiving, and petitions; and in letters through teaching what it means to be a people of God. Most centrally, God is revealed in the Gospels through the teaching, actions, death, and resurrection of Jesus Christ.

In order to grow in the knowledge and love of God we must encounter the presence of God in conjunction with Scripture and other means of grace that convey God's character or identity. In particular, we encounter God through those means of grace John Wesley terms "works of piety," the most important of which are Scripture, the Eucharist, and prayer. It is these means of grace through which God unites spiritual presence with the narrative of God's creative and redemptive activity. It is as we participate in these means of grace in congregational worship, small groups, and personal devotions that we grow in our knowledge and love of God.

As with any relationship, how we approach it is critical. Whereas we bring ourselves to every relationship, coming to know another person requires openness, listening, and receptivity on our part. Relationships are easily derailed by inattention or distorted by manipulation. Our relationship with God can be similarly affected. Instead of coming to God with an open and receptive faith, we can find ourselves simply going through the motions of word, sacrament, and prayer—what Wesley would call a dead formalism. Or, we can approach God primarily to secure divine help to achieve our agendas or attain our desires, rather than have to have God shape our agendas and desires.

With regard to how we approach that relationship through Scripture, Robert Mulholland draws a critical distinction between informational reading and formational reading. Informational reading is "analytical, critical, and judgmental." It treats the text as an "object" for us to "master" through understanding, analysis, and interpretation. Our purpose in reading is often functional, to use the text in a way that solves a problem or meets a perceived need.[8] In this we remain the sole agents; the text itself is passive. We may obtain important and helpful information through this approach, much as we might learn about Luther or Wesley through reading a well-researched biography. But as Mullholland says, "In the informational approach to reading we give assent, mental agreement to abstract conceptualizations; but we do not...tend to involve ourselves personally, intimately, openly, receptively in that which we read."⁹ In other words, although this manner of reading is certainly important and necessary, it is not a means to a relationship with God.

Formational reading is quite different. Instead of being linear it is open to "multiple layers of meaning" in a passage. It permits the text to address us, indeed to searchingly examine our hearts and lives. Instead of using the text "according to our own insight and purposes," we are "shaped by the text."¹⁰ Our approach is not critical and analytical but humble, receptive, and loving. Instead of a "problem-solving mentality...we come to be open to that mystery we call *God*."¹¹ We are, in other words, open to hear God's voice, to be addressed by God. Scripture, then, is not something we use but instead becomes something God uses to transform our lives. It is a means through which we participate in a relationship with God.

Our participation in the Eucharist takes a similar form. It can be simply going through the motions or it can be a religious duty to gain an eternal reward. But as we come with an open and receptive faith, it is an occasion to encounter Christ through power of the Spirit. It is indeed a meal with the risen Christ.

The Eucharist mediates the presence of God in Christ

in and through words, signs, and actions that make manifest God's character. Many Christian traditions today follow the ancient practice of a prayer of thanksgiving that narrates what God has done in creation and redemption, calls upon the power of the Holy Spirit, and points to the promise of new creation. Virtually all Christian traditions retell and reenact the actions of Jesus at the Last Supper, which enables our continued communion with one another and the One who died and rose for the forgiveness of sins and to give new life. The remembrance (*anamnesis*) involved here is not simply cognitive or informational but experiential and participatory. It is a matter of the heart as well as the mind. It involves not only a present experience of what God has done but also a real anticipation of the fullness of all God has promised.

What is true of Scripture and the Eucharist is likewise true of prayer. Prayers can be mere recitals or religious obligations or functional attempts to seek God's aid in meeting our desires. But they are also the most central and common means of relationship with God. When approached with a receptive faith and openness to listen, prayer is a vital means of communication with God and of being in God's presence, so much so that it is an essential component of the Eucharist and is inextricably joined with any formational reading of Scripture.

It is the specificity of prayers that enable their being

prime means of grace. Whenever we enumerate why we are offering praise and thanksgiving to God, we come to know the God we meet in prayer as the one who is all this and more. Whenever we name our petitions and intercessions, we come to know God as the one who cares even more deeply than we do about these concerns and who cannot only act in response but can also illumine our vision to see these needs with greater clarity and empower us to act as well. When we confess our sin, we come to know more deeply the forgiveness and love of God.

This is why, in addition to our own extemporaneous prayers, it is so crucial to pray the prayers of the Christian tradition, beginning with the Lord's Prayer, as well as psalms, hymns, and other forms of music. By expanding the language of prayer beyond that which we would choose, they enable us to know God more fully and deeply.[12]

The Gift of New Life

An open and receptive faith is our primary prerequisite for a transformative relationship with God. Without that faith we close ourselves off from God and go through life unaware of God's presence and untouched by God's redemption in Christ. To put it simply, without faith we cannot have a new heart.

But this claim is not self-evident. There is a long tradition that virtues are in fact cultivated—that is, we acquire them by way of habitual choices we make over time. This view has proved persuasive because it contains much truth. We do not tell a child to say thank you for a gift because the child *is* grateful but because the child *ought* to be grateful. We hope that by saying thank you, the child will, over time, actually become thankful through learning to see receiving a gift as an occasion for gratitude. Likewise, although we may not initially feel hopeful, we can cultivate hopefulness by acting hopefully—that is, by looking at a set of circumstances from the perspective of the gospel and acting accordingly. Doing this over time will make us a hopeful person. The virtue of hope will have become habitual and we will come to naturally envision circumstances in light of our hope in Christ.

My argument does not deny this but places it into a larger relational framework. Whereas our choices and actions do have a formative effect, we do not in the end fundamentally create our own character. We are either shaped by our interaction with cultural values, practices, and understandings in a fallen world or we are being shaped by God through the presence and power of the Holy Spirit in and through the means of grace practiced in the Christian community. There is where we meet God. There is where God's story is told and retold, enacted and reenacted. There, in response to this God, new affections are formed, new desires take root, and new lives are lived.

There persons grow in gratitude for creation and redemption, hope in God's promises, and love for God and for all that is loved by God. There persons learn to look at the world with new eyes.

New life can be cultivated only because it is first received as a gracious gift. This is not a point about chronology. A person may indeed "try out" Christianity through participating in a Christian community and over time come to believe what Christians believe through coming to know God revealed in Jesus Christ. The point here is *theological*: there is a priority of grace in bringing that person to the Christian community and enabling him or her to know God through faith. And it is the resulting gift of new affections in the heart that is foundational for growth in the Christian life.

So the Christian life is a work of God, but it is also a work in progress. We do not suddenly transcend culture overnight. In fact, we do not fully transcend culture at all. At best, we engage in prayerful discernment, at one and the same time seeking to contextualize the gospel while avoiding its domestication, to live out the gospel in our world with faithful effectiveness while avoiding unfaithful compromise.

If growing in the knowledge and love of God occurs within an environment of means of grace, then our participation in worship and a devotional life is critical. That

participation is indeed a choice—at any given occasion
we do it or not—and we are in fact continually presented
with temptations and circumstances that draw us away
from God. Much of this pressure is societal: friends and
family whose assumptions of what desires and motivations
are "normal" or "natural" may conflict with Christian affections; media programming and advertising that might
paint a different meaning for life than that of the gospel;
work and recreation that may encompass practices and
values that lead to a way of life contrary to that of the
kingdom of God. Some of this, as we have seen, can take
root within the church itself.

The problem we face is twofold. First, how do we stay
in relationship with God when faced with such a formidable array of counterpressures? Second, how as Christians
do we navigate our way through the culture as we seek to
live faithfully? I will hold the second question for the next
chapter and address the first one here.

Drawing on a deep tradition of Christian spirituality,
Wesley placed his people in a diverse array of small groups
within which they were held accountable to a spiritual
discipline.[13] The basic pattern was attendance at a weekly
meeting during which they gave an account of how they
were or were not able to keep the discipline during the
previous week. The ensuing discussion provided both encouragement to keep the discipline during the next week

and strategies to avoid being drawn away from God and their neighbor. It enabled them to maintain an open and receptive faith.

Disciplined accountability is as helpful today as it was in the eighteenth century. Those who desire to grow in the knowledge and love of God need a set of practices—practices that both provide encouragement and engender discussion—that holds them accountable to participation in means of grace. Wesley enforced attendance in the small group and faithfulness to the discipline by making them conditions of membership in a Methodist society. Today Christians could form associations for the same purpose through mutual consent and covenant.[14]

Now to sum up the argument of this chapter: conversion bears fruit when it is seen as a beginning, not an ending. It is as we grow in the knowledge and love of God that new affections take firm root in the heart and increasingly direct our desires and motivations. This new life is the work of the Holy Spirit, received through an open and receptive faith and our being in relationship with God. That relationship occurs largely through our participation in means of grace such as Scripture, the Eucharist, and prayer, because it is in these that we simultaneously encounter the presence and identity of God. These means of grace make the Christian community an alternative to the surrounding culture, a pointer and at times a manifestation of the coming kingdom of God. Because the culture tends to pull us away from God toward competing stories, values, and practices, we need a form of disciplined accountability as well as a place for conversation to assist us in remaining in relationship with God.

To be a Christian is to have a new heart with new affections. It enables us to look at the world through new eyes, live in the world with new desires, and act in the world with new motivations. But it is one thing to be motivated by, say, compassion for one's neighbor and another thing to act in a way that is actually compassionate. It is one thing to desire justice and another thing to work for justice.

Holiness of heart does, as Wesley said, lead to holiness of life. The new birth is indeed the necessary precondition for discipleship. But living effectively as disciples is not straightforward and at times not easy. That will be the subject of chapter 7.

Chapter Seven

FREEDOM TO SERVE

In chapter 6 we saw how aspects of our culture can inculcate desires and motivations in the heart contrary to those given in new birth. The pervasive consumerism that marks American culture is a prime example of a cultural norm that can produce in us divided hearts. To grow in love and other Christian affections we need to participate in the spiritual practices of a community that is shaped and governed by the story of God in Christ. It is this participation that helps us remain focused and open to the grace of God in our lives.

But the other case study in chapter 2, that of racism, points to a different problem. Why, if our hearts are disposed to love our neighbor, do we nonetheless fail to actually live and act in ways consistent with that disposition? Michael O. Emerson and Christian Smith concluded that most white evangelicals have inadequate cultural tool kits, and this fatally compromises their actual discipleship. Inadequate knowledge and faulty assumptions combine to block our faithfully living out a new life in Christ.

John Wesley noted that this was an inevitable problem even for those who had attained Christian perfection— that is, those whose hearts were fully and completely motivated and governed by love of God and neighbor.

> The highest perfection which man can attain, while the soul dwells in the body, does not exclude ignorance, and error, and a thousand other infirmities. Now from wrong judgments, wrong words and actions will often necessarily flow: And in some cases, wrong affections also may spring from the same source. I may judge wrong of you; I may think more or less highly of you than I ought to think; and this mistake in my judgment may not only occasion something wrong in my behavior, but it may have a still deeper effect.... From a wrong apprehension, I may love and esteem you either more or less than I ought.[1]

Wesley terms these errors in judgment "involuntary transgressions." Through ignorance or mistake, our actions are contrary to our own best desires and may even produce inappropriate affections.

Although Wesley is correct that we never escape misjudgments in this life, we can nonetheless counteract involuntary transgressions through better information and more accurate assumptions. If the problem of divided hearts discussed in the previous chapter is addressed through avoiding separation from God, the solution to involuntary transgressions lies in overcoming separation from our neighbor.

Demographic Diffusion and Ideological Captivity

Because our culture has a powerful and pervasive impact on what we see—illuminating some things, distorting others, and hiding yet others—we need practices that help us remain open to the Holy Spirit's providing a more accurate and complete vision of the world. The works of piety discussed in the previous chapter meet this need in part because as they serve as means of grace that nurture the growth of Christian affections in the heart, they also enable our growth in the knowledge and love of God. To know God in itself enables our looking upon our world with new eyes.

But complementary to works of piety are what Wesley terms "works of mercy," which are at one and the same time expressions of our love for our neighbor and means of grace that the Spirit uses to further our growth in love. To see how these may help, and some of the forms they may take in our day, we need first to examine two ways our separation from others hinders our ability to love.

The first is global in nature. Churches are necessarily

contextualized in particular cultures and tend to be shaped by the norms and assumptions of those cultures. We see this in the New Testament itself, where the various writers are helping those first Christians navigate their culture faithfully, both in belief and practice. The same dynamic is found in the Old Testament, where prophets forcefully remind Israel what faithful worship and just living require in the midst of a cultural world with radically different assumptions.

The church in America finds itself squarely within a post-Enlightenment Western culture, and as we have seen, often mirrors its prevailing assumptions and norms. The values and perspectives of the market economy, consumerism, romanticist individualism, technology, and the entertainment industry have all shaped how the church as a whole engages in and understands the world.

Western culture has a global sweep in the early twenty-first century. Even so, much of the rest of the world have cultures very distinct from those in the West. Not only is the Western church not the whole of Christianity but also it is no longer the demographic norm. Today the typical Christian is no longer found in Europe or America but in Africa or Latin America.[2]

If we are to see more clearly the world as God sees it, we need practices in the church that will enable us to transcend the limitations that inevitably accompany our living in a particular culture. This will involve coming to know how Christians in other cultures are seeking to live faithfully, as well as attending to the inconsistencies they may see in our attempts to do so. The point is not to uncritically emulate their actions or accept their critique (nor should they ours) but to use it as a way to get a transcultural perspective on how we live out our new life in Christ.

The second form of separation is internal, within America itself. Of course, American cultural diversity is nothing new. Diversity marked prerevolutionary America and has grown in both size and complexity since. For churches in America this has always meant adapting to diverse cultural heritages and in many cases conducting worship and ministry in a host of new languages.

Intermixed with ethnic and racial diversity has been diversity of socioeconomic class and geography. It makes a difference whether one lives in the Northeast or the Midwest, or in an urban core, a suburban residential area, or in rural America. Churches have always adapted to these contexts as well.

As is well known, this process of adapting to new cultures was neither smooth nor consistent. Cultural insensitivity and ignorance marked much of the nineteenth-century missionary endeavors both at home and abroad. Evaluating other cultures through the lens of our own (and often assuming as well the superiority of Western culture) seriously compromised the most well-intentioned efforts. Nonetheless, the churches that emerged began reading the Scriptures for themselves and contextualized the gospel in their own way.[3] In America, the most notable early examples of this were the African American churches.

So in some ways the churches within America mirror the global diversity. Thus the same dynamic is at play: we need a way to help one another see beyond cultural limitations and gain a larger perspective on the world.

As difficult as this problem of internal separation has been for American Christianity, trends in recent decades have made the problem immeasurably worse. Prosperity, demography, and technology are combining to reinforce our internal cultural biases to the point of polarization and rigidity. This change in America is now well documented by many and presented in its most accessible form by journalist Bill Bishop and sociologist Robert G. Cushing.

Empowered by prosperity and the mobility it enables, they argue, Americans "were reordering their lives around their values, their tastes, and their beliefs. They were clustering in communities of like-mindedness."[4] The result was increased homogeneity in neighborhoods, civic clubs, political parties, and churches. As marketing analyst J. Walker Smith says, people "are finding communities that fit their values—where they don't have to live with neighbors or community groups that might force them to compromise their principles or their tastes."[5] The result, says Bishop, is "balkanized communities whose inhabitants find other Americans to be culturally incomprehensible."[6] This is hardly the way for persons to expand their cultural tool kits.

Although he didn't have the benefit of modern sociological analysis, John Wesley was an astute observer of the effects of separation in his own very hierarchical society. He notes:

> One great reason why the rich, in general, have so little sympathy for the poor, is, because they so seldom visit them. Hence it is, that, according to the common observation, one part of the world does not know what the other suffers. Many of them do not know, because they do not care to know; they keep out of the way of knowing it; and then plead their voluntary ignorance as an excuse for their hardness of heart.[7]

The difference between Wesley's society and our own is that in his the separation was "built in" but could be overcome through choosing to do so; in ours we are choosing to segregate ourselves from others.

Separation from others who are unlike ourselves is by itself detrimental to loving our neighbors with faithfulness and effectiveness, but unfortunately it also produces a by-product that makes matters immeasurably worse. As Cass R. Sunstein succinctly puts it, "When people find themselves in groups of like-minded types, they are especially likely to move to extremes."[8] Hundreds of

experiments have consistently confirmed this phenomenon.[9] The perspectives of homogeneous groups are continually reinforced, increasing the intensity with which
they are believed and the rigidity with which they are held.

An important study by Robert Putnam and David
Campbell underscores this point. They emphasize the
critical importance of "religious social networks" for shaping the beliefs and attitudes of persons in local churches.
Speaking particularly of political attitudes, they argue that
persons sort themselves, often unconsciously, into congregations, and even within congregations, with persons like
themselves. "The more one kind of person predominates
within a given congregation," they found, "the more that
others who perceive themselves as similar will feel comfortable there (and those who see themselves as different
will feel uncomfortable, to the point of leaving.)"[10]

It is through religious social networks that people
"receive religiously infused signals" about a range of concerns, political or otherwise. Sometimes this is through
direct conversation, but it is also communicated subtly—
"the joke passed along via e-mail here, an offhand com-
ment there."[11] The result is that religious social networks
become "echo chambers." "Social interaction among like-
minded co-religionists reinforces and even hardens one's
beliefs, even if the process is subtle."[12]

One might think that media and technology would

counteract the insularity of groups. After all, there is a diversity of programming on television and radio and innumerable sources of information and opinions on the Internet and in print. Yet this in fact has the opposite effect. People choose their news sources, programs, books, and blogs, and, as Bishop says, "they self-segregate into their own gated media communities."[13] They filter out in advance perspectives unlike their own and select out or reinterpret information to reinforce their own perspectives. "In short," says Sunstein, "people are motivated to accept accounts that fit with their preexisting convictions; acceptance of those accounts makes them feel better, and acceptance of competing accounts makes them feel worse."[14]

Seeing with New Eyes

If salvation is simply a matter of forgiveness of our sins so that we have a happy eternal destination, then the problem we are raising is peripheral. However desirable, it is not really central to Christian conversion. But if what God is about in salvation is the transformation of hearts and lives so that we love God and our neighbor as we have been loved by God in Christ, then the problem of separation is a serious threat to our living out our salvation. We simply must find ways to break out of cultural captivity so that we see the world more as God sees it.

Perhaps the first step, as both patristic theologians and

John Wesley would insist, is the cultivation of humility. In recommending this they were not calling for a practice of continually demeaning ourselves but for seeing ourselves honestly, as God sees us. This certainly means seeing our sin in increasing clarity. It includes as well seeing our worth and dignity as persons created in God's image and for whom Christ died. But it also involves acknowledging our finitude. We are created, not the Creator, and we necessarily have limited knowledge and perspectives. Yet we also have the potential to increase our knowledge and enlarge our perspectives, enabling us to see our world with increasing accuracy and understanding.

Acknowledging our limitations and our need, and motivated by love, how do we then grow? The key is to have practices in the life of the Christian community that enable us to look at the world through the eyes of others and enlarge the concerns that engage our hearts and inform our prayers for one another. Through such practices we can begin to escape the cultural captivity fostered by separation.

What is needed, then, is a kind of empathy. The definition of empathy is highly contested—C. Daniel Batson has identified eight distinct definitions in neuroscience research alone.[15] It is frequently confused with sympathy (and in eighteenth-century philosophy it was not distinguished from it). Empathy, as I use the term, is a kind of understanding, a capacity to affectively share something of the situation or experience of another. Empathy is feeling *with* another, whereas sympathy is feeling *for* another. Sympathy, unlike empathy, does not in itself require understanding another's condition similarly to the way he or she understands it. I thus agree with Martin Hoffman's careful definition of empathy as "an affective response more appropriate to another's situation than one's own."[16] Without empathy for the suffering or distress of our neighbor, it is difficult for us to be in solidarity with him or her.

Neuroscientists, psychologists, philosophers, and literary theorists debate whether our human capacity for empathy (now believed to be biologically grounded in "mirror neurons") is a source of altruistic or moral behavior. My argument here is not that empathy is a source of compassion (for compassion is a disposition of the heart as described in chapters 5 and 6) but that it is necessary for compassionate and just *action* in the world. Apart from a compassionate heart, empathy may either be restricted to one's nation, race, community, or family, or it can evoke an adverse or apathetic response. But with a heart motivated by love, it can enable compassion to become manifest as acts of caring and justice.

What is needed, then, is to identify practices that enable persons growing in love to understand the world through the eyes of others. We have as an initial clue this statement by Suzanne Keen, who has written extensively on how novels evoke empathy in their readers: "Empathy, a vicarious, spontaneous sharing of affect, can be provoked by witnessing another's emotional state, by hearing about another's condition, or even by reading."[17] We also have the important observation of Emerson and Smith, cited earlier, on the importance of interracial friendships for adding resources to one's cultural tool kit and enabling one to become more aware of how injustice can take structural and systemic form.

So let's begin with the obvious: one practice is listening to the stories of persons different from ourselves.[18] This can be done indirectly, through books, documentaries, movies, and other media. The hope is that this will enable us to begin to understand and to a slight degree even experience the world as they do. We can then meditate on what is read or heard, opening our hearts and minds for God to enlighten our understanding. This also can occur as a group discussion around a common reading or movie, again grounded in and suffused with prayer.

A more direct practice is engaging in actual conversation in which participants are able to share something of themselves and their story. This works best as a series of conversations over time. Engagement in conversation over time is potentially more helpful, as it enables growth in understanding over time. But its possibility for enlarging our vision is premised on our coming to those conversations with an openness motivated by love and shaped by humility.

Friendship takes the conversational approach much deeper. As Douglas Powe says, "[Friendship] implies a relationship that moves beyond mere acquaintance toward some form of mutuality with another. This mutuality is based upon seeing the other and hearing the other without having to recreate the other into one's own image."[19]

Emerson and Smith showed how interracial friendships could decisively expand our cultural tool kits. But they also showed how rare such friendships are. They are rare because they are difficult. Several stories of friendships between white and black evangelicals were published in the 1990s.[20] What is striking about these accounts is, in spite of their desires, how difficult and at times painful they found real interracial friendship to be. Yet all testify that, for all the difficulties they faced along the way, they found their friendships were genuine means of grace, used by God to enable their growth in love and their greater faithfulness in ministry.

Douglas Powe recommends engaging friendships as an initial step toward racial and gender reconciliation. The advantage of friendship is that it enables both parties to be themselves, and to be valued for themselves, apart from cultural biases that privilege one over another, "An engaging friendship," says Powe, "is based upon valuing the friendship itself and caring for one's friend. It is this understanding of friendship that gets us closer to a love of neighbor that models God's justice and not just our own interest."[21]

The best way for friendship to develop is when persons or local churches engage in a common project. Bill Bishop warns that "simply putting two groups together" does not automatically lead to mutual respect—indeed, it can "result in *increased* tension and discrimination."[22] Mere acquaintance with another, without the benefit of a longer-term relationship, can actually perpetuate misunderstanding.

This may be why Promise Keepers, for all of Coach McCartney's good intentions, failed at the goal of racial reconciliation. The interracial contact was limited to one intense event; as a first step it was fine, but as a one-time occurrence it was ineffectual. Compare that with an interracial football team. Here a group of diverse men engage in a common task over time and get to know one another as they work together. This was the actual experience that underlay McCartney's concern for racial reconciliation in the church.

Whereas many important and worthwhile activities of local churches involve encountering persons unlike themselves, some involve partnering with others on common projects. Volunteers in mission projects often have groups from local churches traveling to another area in America or another country where there is a need and partnering with local Christians to meet that need. Although these are short-term missions, working and worshiping with others, hearing their stories, and experiencing something of their lives, transforms the perspectives of those who go. Moreover, their testimonies in turn have an impact on others in their church back home.

Growing numbers of churches are partnering together on a longer-term basis to meet a range of needs in rural or urban contexts. Often this involves a church from outside a community partnering with a church in the community for common ministry. When these partnerships cross racial or socioeconomic lines, there is potential for growth in understanding. Of course, the reason for the partnership is to collaborate on meeting agreed-upon needs—the expansion of cultural tool kits is a happy by-product of the partnership. But its effect is transformative and lasting. All this presupposes, however, that the churches engage in the partnership as equals and that persons from outside the community are willing to listen and learn from those within the community.[23]

We can never fully overcome our ignorance of many things, but we can take concrete steps to look at the world through the eyes of others, especially Christians who are different from us. Intentional listening, conversations and friendship over time, and partnerships in ministry are among the ways that God can use to broaden and deepen our understanding and enable us to act more in accordance with the love that is in our hearts.

A Future for Love

The greatest danger to our freedom is thinking we are free when we really are not. What seems only natural in our culture may not be so in the kingdom of God. What seems good and right to us may in fact be contrary to the will of God. Wrong desires and limited understanding conspire to hold us in a captivity in which we are free to do almost anything except love as God loves.

As we have seen, there are really two threats that the individualist and romanticist kind of freedom poses to the Christian life. The first is when out of our desires we project the God we want—a domesticated deity who affirms but never questions, who confronts but never challenges, who supports our agendas without calling us into mission.[24] In truth, most of us who say we follow Christ have divided hearts, in part faithfully responding to the God revealed in Christ, but in part recreating God into a more amenable divinity. We want to love God, but we also want to hold on to that illusory freedom and those desires of the heart that God seems to threaten. We come close to God, yet at the same time keep our distance. As long as we remain halfway Christians, we can never be the persons we were created to be.

The way to true freedom is to grow in both the knowledge and the love of God. Our continued separation from God must be overcome. That occurs through a transforming relationship with God, in and through means of grace that convey God's nature and story even as they enable us to encounter God's presence. The God we meet in this way is not the projection of our disordered desires but the God who is other than us,[25] who has acted for our redemption and who is known most fully in the life, death, and resurrection of Jesus Christ. To know and love *this* God over time is to acquire deeply rooted holy affections such that love increasingly governs our desires and motivations.

If the first threat has to do with remaining sin, the second has to do with our finitude. Our knowledge is limited; our understanding is inadequate; our judgments are flawed. The particularity of our culture reinforces our limited perspective. Even if we have love for our neighbors, our misconstrual of their motivations or the situations in which they find themselves leads us to ineffectual or even harmful actions. Our actions subvert our love, and God's mission in the world is hindered.

Here the way to true freedom is to gain an enlarged perspective. Our cultural separation from our neighbor must be overcome. That occurs through relationships with others that enable us to hear their stories and see the world through their eyes. The practices that enable us to do this are means of grace that God uses to give us new vision, through which we continually grow in our ability to see the world as God sees it, and to act accordingly. In this way love becomes effectively embodied in our actions.

Love can be made manifest in the world because of what God has done in Jesus Christ and continues to do through the Holy Spirit. That is, the reality of love is a gift of grace. In the end, all of creation will be fully renewed and transformed in love. But even now, on this side of that eschaton, there is a future for love, because God is already giving persons new hearts and new vision and setting them free to participate in God's mission of renewing the creation in love.

NOTES

1. The Shaping of Evangelical Theology

1. See my discussion in Henry H. Knight III, *A Future for Truth* (Nashville: Abingdon Press, 1997), 18–19. On characteristic evangelical beliefs see Alister McGrath, *Evangelicalism and the Future of Christianity* (Downers Grove, Ill.: InterVarsity, 1995), 55–56; on evangelical spirituality see Stanley J. Grenz, *Revisioning Evangelical Theology* (Downers Grove, Ill.: InterVarsity, 1993), 30–31.

2. Knight, *Future for Truth*, 22–35.

3. The case is ably made by Douglas A. Sweeney, *The American Evangelical Story* (Grand Rapids: Baker , 2005). It underlies the five-volume *History of Evangelicalism*, the first volume of which is the excellent account by Mark A. Noll, *The Rise of Evangelicalism: The Age of Edwards, Whitefield and the Wesleys* (Downers Grove, Ill.: InterVarsity, 2003).

4. See for example Donald W. Dayton, "Some Doubts about the Usefulness of the Category 'Evangelical'" in *The*

Variety of American Evangelicalism, ed. Donald W. Dayton and Robert K. Johnston (Downers Grove, Ill.: InterVarsity, 1991), 245–51.

5. David W. Bebbington, *Evangelicalism in Modern Britain: A History from the 1730s to the 1880s* (Grand Rapids: Baker), 2–3.

6. Roger E. Olson, *Reformed and Always Reforming* (Grand Rapids: Baker, 2007), 43.

7. Peter Goodwin Heltzel, *Jesus & Justice* (New Haven: Yale University Press, 2009), 7.

8. Thomas S. Kidd, *The Great Awakening* (New Haven: Yale University Press, 2009), xiv.

9. Kilian McDonnell, "The Experiential and the Social: New Models from the Pentecostal/Roman Catholic Dialogue," *One in Christ* 9 (1973): 48; cited in Steven J. Land, *Pentecostal Spirituality* (1993; reprinted Cleveland, Tenn.: CPT, 2010), 38.

10. On this see Ellen T. Charry, *By the Renewing of Your Minds: The Pastoral Function of Christian Doctrine* (New York: Oxford University Press, 1999).

11. Avihu Zakai, *Jonathan Edwards's Philosophy of History* (Princeton: Princeton University Press, 2003), 32.

12. For an extensive discussion of Wesley's understanding of faith as a spiritual sense and its implications for experience see Theodore Runyon, *The New Creation: John Wesley's Theology Today* (Nashville: Abingdon Press, 1998), chapter 5.

13. John Wesley, "An Earnest Appeal to Men of Reason

and Religion," par. 6, in *The Appeals to Men of Reason and Religion*, vol. 11 of *The Works of John Wesley*, ed. Gerald R. Cragg (Nashville: Abingdon Press, 1975), 45.

14. Jonathan Edwards, "A Faithful Narrative," in *The Works of Jonathan Edwards*, vol. 4, *The Great Awakening*, ed. C. C. Goen (New Haven: Yale University Press, 1972), 144–212.

15. See *The Works of Jonathan Edwards*, vol. 2, *Religious Affections*, ed. John E. Smith (New Haven: Yale University Press, 1959).

16. See for example John Wesley, "The General Spread of the Gospel," in *Sermons II*, vol. 2 of *The Works of John Wesley*, ed. Albert C. Outler (Nashville: Abingdon Press, 1982).

17. On this see Timothy J. Crutcher, *The Crucible of Life: The Role of Experience in John Wesley's Theological Method* (Lexington, Ky.: Emeth, 2010).

18. For more extended discussion and critique of these methods of apologetics, see Knight, *Future for Truth*, 45–49. Examples of evidentialist apologetics include John Warwick Montgomery, *History and Christianity* (Minneapolis: Bethany House, 1964), and *Faith Founded on Fact* (Nashville: Thomas Nelson, 1978), as well as R. C. Sproul et al., *Classical Apologetics: A Rational Defense of the Christian Faith and Critique of Presuppositional Apologetics* (Grand Rapids: Zondervan, 1984). On the popular level is Josh McDowell, *Evidence That Demands a Verdict* (San Bernardino, Calif.: Campus Crusade for Christ, 1972), and Lee Strobel, *The Case for Christ* (Grand Rapids: Zondervan, 1998). Examples of presuppositionalist apologetics include Ronald H. Nash, *The Word of God and the Mind of Man* (Grand Rapids: Zondervan, 1982), and Carl F. H.

Henry, *Toward a Recovery of Christian Belief* (Wheaton: Crossway, 1990).

19. For an extended discussion of this "transformationist evangelical" trajectory in its Wesleyan and pentecostal forms see Henry H. Knight III, ed., *From Aldersgate to Azusa Street* (Eugene, Oreg.: Wipf and Stock, 2011).

20. On Pietism see Dale Brown, *Understanding Pietism* (Grand Rapids: Eerdmans, 1978); F. Ernest Stoeffler, *The Rise of Evangelical Pietism* (Leiden: E. J. Brill, 1965); and Carter Lindberg, ed., *The Pietist Theologians* (Malden, Mass.: Blackwell, 2004).

21. On the Moravian Brethren, besides the books on Pietism listed above, see Arthur J. Freeman, *An Ecumenical Theology of the Heart: The Theology of Count Nicholas Ludwig Von Zinzendorf* (n.p.: Moravian Church in America, 1998).

22. For the awakening in America generally, see Michael J. Crawford, *Seasons of Grace* (New York: Oxford University Press, 1991); on Edwards see the magnificent biography by George M. Marsden, *Jonathan Edwards: A Life* (New Haven: Yale University Press, 2003). A good survey of Anglican evangelical parish priests is Albert Brown-Lawson, *John Wesley and the Anglican Evangelicals of the Eighteenth Century* (Edinburgh: Pentland, 1994). A fascinating study of the Scottish awakening and its impact on the camp meeting tradition in America is Leigh Eric Schmidt, *Holy Fairs: Scottish Communion and American Revivals in the Early Modern Period* (Princeton: Princeton University Press, 1989).

23. On Wesley's Methodism see Richard P. Heitzenrater, *Wesley and the People Called Methodists* (Nashville: Abingdon

Press, 1993), and Henry D. Rack, *Reasonable Enthusiast: John Wesley and the Rise of Methodism* (London: Epworth, 2002). On George Whitefield see Harry S. Stout, *The Divine Dramatist* (Grand Rapids: Eerdmans, 1991), and Frank Lambert, *"Peddlar in Divinity"* (Princeton: Princeton University Press, 1994). On another significant segment of Calvinistic Methodism see Alan Harding, *The Countess of Huntingdon's Connection* (New York: Oxford University Press, 2003).

24. Wesley, "An Earnest Appeal," par. 2, 45.

25. Such holiness denominations today include the Wesleyan Church, the Free Methodists, the Salvation Army, the Church of the Nazarene, the Church of God (Anderson, Indiana), and the Christian and Missionary Alliance. These all trace their origins to the nineteenth-century holiness movement. A fine history of the movement is Melvin E. Dieter, *The Holiness Revival of the Nineteenth Century* (Metuchen, N.J.: Scarecrow, 1980).

26. American Pentecostal denominations include the Church of God in Christ, the Church of God (Cleveland, Tennessee), the Pentecostal Holiness Church, the United Holy Church of America, the Assemblies of God, and the International Church of the Foursquare Gospel. On the history of pentecostal and charismatic movements see the excellent survey by Vinson Synan, *The Holiness-Pentecostal Tradition* (Grand Rapids: Eerdmans, 1977).

27. A good survey of the charismatic movement in America that keeps these issues in mind is Charles E. Hummel, *Fire in the Fireplace: Charismatic Renewal in the Nineties* (Downers Grove: InterVarsity, 1993).

28. Independent charismatics most notably include the "Word of Faith" churches, with a health-and-prosperity teaching. Another significant group is comprised of "Third Wave" churches, which include evangelicals previously resistant to charismatic phenomena and which seek to integrate "word and power"; the Vineyard churches are perhaps the best known of the Third Wave charismatics.

29. On the adoption of the *imago Dei* in mission theology, and for surveys of missions in general, see David J. Bosch, *Transforming Mission: Paradigm Shifts in the Theology of Mission* (Maryknoll, N.Y.: Orbis, 1991), and James A. Scherer, *Gospel, Church and Kingdom* (Minneapolis: Augsburg, 1987).

30. A good survey of evangelical missions can be found in Sweeny, *American Evangelical Story*, chapter 4.

31. See my discussion of contextualization in Knight, *Future for Truth*, 131–37. Other discussions that are helpful include Lesslie Newbigin, *The Gospel in a Pluralist Society* (Grand Rapids: Eerdmans, 1989), 148–51; Orlando Costas, *Christ Outside the Gate* (Maryknoll, N.Y.: Orbis, 1982); Rene Padilla, *Mission between the Times* (Grand Rapids: Eerdmans, 1985); and William A. Dyrness, *Learning about Theology from the Third World* (Grand Rapids: Eerdmans, 1990).

32. For a brief but thorough discussion of orthodoxy, orthopraxy, and orthopathy see the introduction in Richard B. Steele, ed., *"Heart Religion" in the Methodist Tradition and Related Movements* (Lanham, Md.: Scarecrow, 2001), xxx–xxxv. Among the theologians arguing for an integration of these three terms (but not necessarily defining them in exactly the same way) are Richard J. B. Steele, Randy L. Maddox, Gregory S. Clapper (who uses *orthokardia* instead of *orthopathy*), Steven

J. Land, Theodore Runyon, Cheryl Bridges Johns, and Samuel Solivan (*orthopathos*).

33. See my discussion of the Holy Spirit and Scripture in Knight, *Future for Truth,* 109–16.

2. The Modern Quest for Freedom

1. Charles Taylor, *Sources of the Self: The Making of the Modern Identity* (Cambridge, Mass.: Harvard University Press, 1989), 315.

2. Ibid., 310.

3. Ibid., 14.

4. Ibid. Charles Taylor provides a comprehensive and rich account of their development over time and their many permutations in *Sources of the Self.*

5. Ibid., 143–44 and 168.

6. Robert N. Bellah et al., *Habits of the Heart: Individualism and Commitment in American Life* (Berkeley: University of California Press, 1985), 33. Bellah's colleagues are Richard Madsen, William M. Sullivan, Ann Swidler, and Steven M. Tipton. It should be said in Franklin's defense that he had a lifelong commitment to civic responsibility and the betterment of the community.

7. Darrell L. Guder, ed., *Missional Church: A Vision for the Sending of the Church in North America* (Grand Rapids: Eerdmans, 1998), 29. Guder's colleague, Craig Van Gelder, drafted the chapter cited here.

8. Taylor, *Sources,* 384.

9. Ibid., 374.

10. Bellah, *Habits*, 34.

11. Christian Smith and three colleagues have recently shown how pervasive this expressive individualism is among American youth in *Lost in Transition: The Dark Side of Emerging Adulthood* (New York: Oxford University Press, 2011). Among their findings were that youths understand morality as a matter of personal choice, decided by what "feels" right, and that they were unable to see any downside to consumerism.

12. Michael O. Emerson and Christian Smith, *Divided by Faith: Evangelical Religion and the Problem of Race in America* (New York: Oxford University Press, 2000), 7.

13. Ibid., 9.

14. Ibid., ix.

15. Spencer Perkins and Chris Rice, *More Than Equals: Racial Healing for the Sake of the Gospel* (Downers Grove, Ill.: InterVarsity, 1993), 27.

16. Emerson, *Divided by Faith*, 11.

17. Amos Yong, *The Spirit Poured Out on All Flesh: Pentecostalism and the Possibility of Global Theology* (Grand Rapids: Baker, 2005), 56.

18. Ibid., 57.

19. Emerson, *Divided by Faith*, 54. They are here drawing on George Yancey's analysis in *Beyond Black and White: Reflections on Racial Reconciliation* (Grand Rapids: Baker, 1996).

20. Ibid., 55.

21. Ibid., 58–59.

22. Ibid., 76.

23. Ibid., 76–77.

24. Ibid., 77.

25. Ibid., 78–79.

26. Ibid., 18.

27. Murray Jardine, *The Making and Unmaking of Technological Society* (Grand Rapids: Baker, 2004), 26.

28. Ibid., 16.

29. Ibid., 55.

30. Ibid., 89.

31. Ibid.

32. John Wesley, "The Causes of the Inefficacy of Christianity," par. 17, in *Sermons IV*, vol. 4 of *The Works of John Wesley* (Nashville: Abingdon Press, 1987), 95–96.

33. Ibid.

34. Robert Wuthnow, *Christianity in the 21st Century* (New York: Oxford University Press, 1993), 192.

35. Ibid., 195.

36. Ibid., 196–97.

37. Ibid., 196.

38. Sam Van Eman, *On Earth as It Is in Advertising* (Grand Rapids: Baker, 2005), 16.

39. Jardine, *Technological Society*, 124.

40. Wuthnow, *21st Century*, 200.

41. Van Eman, *Advertising*, 11.

42. John G. Stackhouse Jr., *Humble Apologetics: Defending the Faith Today* (New York: Oxford University Press, 2002), 62–63.

43. Rodney Clapp, *Families at the Crossroads* (Downers Grove, Ill.: InterVarsity, 1993), 91.

44. Van Eman, *Advertising*, 122.

45. Wuthnow, *21st Century*, 202.

46. Christian Smith and Michael O. Emerson, *Passing the Plate: Why American Christians Don't Give Away More Money* (New York; Oxford University Press, 2008), 144–45.

3. Freedom in Postmodern Culture

1. Henry H. Knight III, *A Future for Truth* (Nashville: Abingdon Press, 1997), 56–60.

2. Alan Wolfe, *The Transformation of American Religion: How We Actually Live Our Faith* (New York: Free Press, 2003), 2–3.

3. Ibid., 74.

4. Ibid., 187.

5. Ibid., 184.

6. Ibid., 4.

7. "Walking the Old, Old Talk: The Cultural Success of Evangelicalism Is Its Greatest Weakness," *Christianity Today* 47, no. 10 (2003): 334–35.

8. Wolfe, *Transformation*, 184.

9. Ibid., 94.

10. Robert Wuthnow, "How Small Groups Are Transform-

ing Our Lives," *Christianity Today* 38, no. 2 (1994): 22. This article is adapted from Robert Wuthnow, *Sharing the Journey* (New York: Free Press, 1994).

11. Ibid., 23.

12. Ibid.

13. I discuss the epistemological issues more thoroughly in *A Future for Truth*, chapters 2–4.

14. Alasdair MacIntyre, *After Virtue* (Notre Dame: University of Notre Dame Press, 1981), 8.

15. Ibid., 11.

16. Ibid., 23.

17. Ibid., 32.

18. Ibid., 50.

19. Ibid., 52. MacIntyre goes on to examine Bentham's failed attempt to develop a new teleology for moral theory derived from human psychology, and Kant's failed attempt to ground morality in a categorical imperative.

20. Ibid., 60.

21. Ibid., 68.

4. The Particularity of the Presence of God

1. Colin E. Gunton, *The Promise of Trinitarian Theology* (Edinburgh: T & T Clark, 1991), 162.

2. Colin E. Gunton, *Act & Being* (Grand Rapids: Eerdmans, 2002), 1.

3. Ibid., 17.

4. Ibid., 18.

5. Ibid., 65.

6. Ibid., 77.

7. Ibid., 97.

8. Stanley J. Grenz, *The Named God and the Question of Being: A Trinitarian Theo-Ontology* (Louisville: Westminster John Knox, 2005), 133.

9. Ibid., 249.

10. Ibid., 7.

11. Ibid., 283.

12. Ibid.

13. Ibid., 170.

14. Ibid., 207.

15. Ibid., 11.

16. Ibid., 281.

17. Ibid., 326.

18. Ibid., 321.

19. Ibid., 338.

20. David Willis, *Notes on the Holiness of God* (Grand Rapids: Eerdmans, 2002), 1.

21. See William Placher, *The Domestication of Transcendence* (Louisville: Westminster John Knox, 1996), and my discussion in *A Future for Truth* (Nashville: Abingdon Press, 1997), 167–68.

22. Willis, *Holiness of God*, 2.

23. For a comprehensive analysis of modes of divine presence in the Old Testament see Terence E. Fretheim, *The Suffering of God* (Philadelphia: Fortress, 1984), chapter 5.

24. My goal in this section was simply to sketch the nature of incarnational presence rather than provide an extensive discussion. In *A Future for Truth* I provide a more detailed analysis and proposal in chapter 8. For book-length treatments of the atonement with which I in large measure concur see Colin E. Gunton, *The Actuality of Atonement* (Grand Rapids: Eerdmans, 1989), and Robert Sherman, *King, Priest, and Prophet: A Trinitarian Theology of Atonement* (New York: T & T Clark, 2004).

25. I am indebted to Steven J. Land for this important insight.

5. The Transformation of the Heart

1. See for example Gordon T. Smith, *Beginning Well: Christian Conversion & Authentic Transformation* (Downers Grove, Ill.: InterVarsity, 2001). This is a careful and most insightful analysis. My approach comes at conversion from a somewhat different direction by emphasizing Christian affections. For a perceptive account from a Wesleyan perspective see George E. Morris, *The Mystery and Meaning of Conversion* (Nashville: World Methodist Evangelism Press, 2004).

2. Jonathan Edwards, *A Treatise Concerning Religious Affections*, part 1, introductory paragraphs, in John E. Smith, ed., *The Works of Jonathan Edwards*, vol. 2 (New Haven: Yale University Press, 1959), 95.

3. John Wesley, "On Charity," par. III.12, in Albert C. Outler, ed., *The Works of John Wesley*, vol. 3 (Nashville: Abingdon Press, 1986), 306.

4. The two most thorough examinations of affections and tempers in Wesley's theology are Gregory S. Clapper, *John Wesley on Religious Affections* (Metuchen, N.J.: Scarecrow, 1989), and Richard B. Steele, *"Gracious Affections" and "True Virtue" According to Jonathan Edwards and John Wesley* (Metuchen, N.J.: Scarecrow, 1994). Both of these works also address Edwards's usage as well. Clapper understands the two terms to be synonymous in Wesley. For accounts that consider the terms distinct yet related, see Kenneth J. Collins, "John Wesley's Topography of the Heart: Dispositions, Tempers, and Affections," *Methodist History* 36, no. 3 (April 1998): 162–75, and Randy L. Maddox, *Responsible Grace* (Nashville: Abingdon Press, 1994), 69–70. Those who distinguish them in Wesley's theology understand the beginnings of a motivating disposition to be the affection and the enduring or habitual disposition to be the temper.

5. Alasdair MacIntyre, *After Virtue* (Notre Dame: University of Notre Dame Press, 1981).

6. See for example Stanley Hauerwas, *The Peaceable Kingdom* (Notre Dame: Notre Dame University Press, 1991), and *A Community of Character* (Notre Dame: Notre Dame University Press, 1981); Jonathan R. Wilson, *Gospel Virtues* (Downers Grove, Ill.: InterVarsity, 1998), and *Living Faithfully in a Fragmented World* (Harrisburg, Pa.: Trinity Press International, 1998).

7. Robert C. Solomon, *The Passions: Emotions and the Meaning of Life* (Indianapolis: Hackett Publishing, 1993), a

revision to the original 1976 edition, and *True to Our Feelings* (New York: Oxford University Press, 2007); Martha C. Nussbaum, *Upheavals of Thought: The Intelligence of Emotions* (Cambridge: Cambridge University Press, 2001); Robert C. Roberts, *Emotions: An Essay in Aid of Moral Psychology* (Cambridge: Cambridge University Press, 2003).

8. Solomon, *Passions*, 9–12.

9. Ibid., viii–ix.

10. Roberts, *Emotions*, 79.

11. Robert C. Roberts, *Spiritual Emotions: A Psychology of Christian Virtues* (Grand Rapids: Eerdmans, 2007), 11.

12. Ibid., 12.

13. Ibid., 17.

14. A point emphasized by Steven J. Land in *Pentecostal Spirituality: A Passion for the Kingdom* (1993; reprint Cleveland, Tenn.: CPT, 2010).

15. Roberts, *Spiritual Emotions*, 30.

16. Ibid., 29.

17. Ibid., 8.

18. Ibid., 9. Roberts considers other virtues or fruit of the Spirit, such as perseverance, patience, and self-control, as "strengths." See his *The Strengths of a Christian* (Philadelphia: Westminster, 1984).

19. Roberts, *Spiritual Emotions*, 29.

20. Don E. Saliers, *The Soul in Paraphrase: Prayer and the Religious Affections* (New York: Seabury, 1980), 7.

21. Ibid., 8.

22. Ibid., 29.

23. Ibid., 18–19.

24. Ibid., 9.

25. John Wesley, *A Plain Account of Christian Perfection,* par. 19, in *The Works of John Wesley, A. M.,* vol. 9 (Grand Rapids: Baker, 1996), 395.

26. See Smith, *Beginning Well.* Smith's categories are: intellectual, penitential, affective, volitional, sacramental, charismatic, and communal.

27. George W. Stroup, *The Promise of Narrative Theology* (Atlanta: John Knox, 1981), 170.

28. Ibid., 171.

29. Ibid., 174.

30. Ibid., 171.

31. James E. Loder, *The Transforming Moment: Understanding Convictional Experiences* (San Francisco: Harper & Row, 1981).

32. Cheryl Bridges Johns, "From Strength to Strength: The Neglected Role of Crisis in Wesleyan and Pentecostal Discipleship," *Wesleyan Theological Journal* 39, no. 1 (Spring 2004): 146.

33. Ibid., 147.

34. Ibid.

35. Ibid.

36. Could someone grow up in the life of the church and

never need conversion? This is best addressed by looking at what conversion is meant to produce: new understanding, loving relationships with God and neighbor, and holy affections. If these are present and growing, then conversion would not be necessary. However, because one remains embedded in culture, there will still be conflict, a collision of narratives, and a lifelong need to continually experience and appropriate the gospel.

37. Helmut Thielicke, *The Evangelical Faith*, vol. 1 (Grand Rapids: Eerdmans, 1974), 152.

38. See my discussion of this in *A Future for Truth* (Nashville: Abingdon Press, 1997), 71–75.

6. Set Free to Love

1. John Wesley, "The Danger of Riches," in *Sermons III*, vol. 3 of *The Works of John Wesley*, ed. Albert C. Outler (Nashville: Abingdon Press, 1986), 106 ff.

2. Philip D. Kenneson, *Life on the Vine* (Downer's Grove, Ill.: InterVarsity, 1999), 45.

3. Ibid.

4. Ibid., 45.

5. Ibid., 46.

6. Henry H. Knight III, *A Future for Truth* (Nashville: Abingdon Press, 1997), 140–44.

7. Ibid., 99–102.

8. M. Robert Mulholland Jr., *Shaped by the Word*, rev. ed. (Nashville: The Upper Room, 2000), 52–53.

9. Ibid., 55.

10. Ibid., 56–57.

11. Ibid., 59.

12. For a comprehensive examination of how worship in its many aspects shapes Christian affections, see Kendra G. Hotz and Matthew T. Mathews, *Shaping the Christian Life* (Louisville: Westminister John Knox, 2006). For the role of prayer in shaping the affections, see Don E. Saliers, *The Soul in Paraphrase* (New York: Seabury, 1980).

13. Among the most helpful discussions of Wesley's small groups (the classes and bands) and his spiritual discipline are Howard A. Snyder, *Signs of the Spirit* (Grand Rapids: Zondervan, 1989); David Lowes Watson, *The Early Methodist Class Meeting* (Nashville: Discipleship Resources, 1985); David Michael Henderson, *John Wesley's Class Meetings: A Model for Making Disciples* (Nappanee, Ind.: Evangel, 1997); Sondra Matthaei, *Making Disciples: Faith Formation in the Wesleyan Tradition* (Nashville: Abingdon Press, 2000); and Kevin M. Watson, *A Blueprint for Discipleship: Wesley's General Rules as a Guide for Christian Living* (Nashville: Discipleship Resources, 2009).

14. One example would be the Covenant Discipleship groups in contemporary United Methodism. See Steven W. Manskar, *Accountable Discipleship: Living in God's Household* (Nashville: Discipleship Resources, 2003).

7. Freedom to Serve

1. John Wesley, "On Perfection," in *Sermons III*, vol. 3 of *The Works of John Wesley*, ed. Albert C. Outler (Nashville: Abingdon Press, 1986), 73.

2. See Philip Jenkins, *The Next Christendom: The Coming Global Christianity*, 3rd. ed. (New York: Oxford University Press, 2011).

3. On this see Lamin Sanneh, *Translating the Message: The Missionary Impact on Culture* (Maryknoll, N.Y.: Orbis, 2009).

4. Bill Bishop, *The Big Sort: Why the Clustering of Like-Minded America Is Tearing Us Apart* (Boston: Houghton Mifflin, 2008), 13.

5. J. Walker Smith, Ann Clurman, and Craig Wood, *Coming to Concurrence* (Evanston, Ill.: Racom Communications, 2005), 83; cited in Bishop, *Big Sort*, 14.

6. Bishop, *Big Sort*, 14.

7. John Wesley, "On Visiting the Sick" in *Works*, vol. 3, 387–88.

8. Cass R. Sunstein, *Going to Extremes: How Like Minds Unite and Divide* (New York: Oxford University Press, 2009), 2.

9. Bishop, *Big Sort*, 67.

10. Robert D. Putnam and David E. Campbell, *American Grace: How Religion Divides and Unites Us* (New York: Simon & Schuster, 2010), 442.

11. Ibid., 436.

12. Ibid., 437.

13. Bishop, *Big Sort*, 74.

14. Sunstein, *Going to Extremes*, 110.

15. C. Daniel Batson, "These Things Called Empathy: Eight Related but Distinct Phenomena," in Jean Decety and

William Ickes, eds., *The Social Neuroscience of Empathy* (Boston: The MIT Press, 2011), 1 ff.

16. Martin Hoffman, *Empathy and Moral Development: Implications for Caring and Justice* (Cambridge, Mass.: Cambridge University Press, 2011), 4.

17. Suzanne Keen, *Empathy and the Novel* (New York: Oxford University Press, 2010), 4. It should be noted, however, that there are psychological approaches that insist empathy is only possible in face-to-face encounters. For a presentation of this point of view in creative engagement with Wesleyan theology, see M. Kathryn Armistead, "Empathy: A Bridge between Wesleyan Theology and Self Psychology," in M. Kathryn Armistead, Brad D. Strawn, and Ronald W. Wright, eds., *Wesleyan Theology and Social Science: The Dance of Practical Divinity and Discovery* (Newcastle upon Tyne, U.K.: Cambridge Scholars Publishing, 2010), 53 ff. See also chapter 3 in M. Kathryn Armistead, *God-Images in the Healing Process* (Minneapolis: Fortress, 1995).

18. For two African American perspectives, read Edward Gilbreath, *Reconciliation Blues* (Downers Grove, Ill.: InterVarsity, 2007), and William E. Panell, *The Coming Race Wars: A Cry for Reconciliation* (Grand Rapids: Zondervan, 1993).

19. F. Douglas Powe, *Just Us or Justice? Moving toward a Pan-Methodist Theology* (Nashville: Abingdon Press, 2009), 105.

20. See for example Spencer Perkins and Chris Rice, *More Than Equals: Racial Healing for the Sake of the Gospel* (Downers Grove, Ill.: InterVarsity, 1993), and Raleigh Washington and Glen Kehrein, *Breaking Down Walls: A Model for Reconciliation in an Age of Racial Strife* (Chicago: Moody, 1993).

21. Powe, *Just Us or Justice?* 123.

22. Bishop, *Big Sort,* 284–85.

23. For more extensive advice on partnerships in ministry, including but not limited to partnership of local churches, see Ronald J. Snider, Philip N. Olson, and Heidi Rolland Unruh, *Churches That Make a Difference* (Grand Rapids: Baker, 2002), chap. 11; and Ronald J. Sider et al., *Linking Arms, Linking Lives: How Urban-Suburban Partnerships Can Change Communities* (Grand Rapids: Baker, 2008). For another important perspective focused on interracial partnerships in ministry, see Brenda Salter McNeil and Rick Richardson, *The Heart of Racial Justice: How Soul Change Leads to Social Change* (Downers Grove, Ill.: InterVarsity, 2004).

24. This seems to be the prevailing image of God in today's American culture according to sociologists. Yet we still see persons who hold to the opposite image of an angry and condemning God, an image much more culturally prevalent two centuries ago. As this book argues, neither of these adequately reflect the revelation of God in Christ.

25. I'm referring here to disordered affections or tempers as described in earlier chapters. My concern in this book has been largely with sociocultural influences that shape our hearts and vision of God. But both Christian spiritual traditions and modern psychology have also described how our human tendency to project images of God is evoked through personal experiences. For a perceptive discussion of their complexity from a psychological perspective, see M. Kathryn Armistead, *God-Images in the Healing Process.* My argument here is that,

through the presence of the Holy Spirit, in the means of grace we actually have a transformative encounter with the living God and our images of God are shaped in accordance with that divine reality over time as we grow in the knowledge and love of God.

CPSIA information can be obtained at www.ICGtesting.com
Printed in the USA
LVOW101704160912

298900LV00002B/2/P

9 780687 660331